Public School Safety

ALSO BY JOSEPH P. HESTER

*The Ten Commandments: A Handbook of
Religious, Legal and Social Issues*
(McFarland, 2003)

Public School Safety

A Handbook, with a Resource Guide

JOSEPH P. HESTER

McFarland & Company, Inc., Publishers
Jefferson, North Carolina, and London

Library of Congress Cataloguing-in-Publication Data

Hester, Joseph P.
    Public school safety : a handbook, with a resource guide
/ Joseph P. Hester.
       p.   cm.
    Includes bibliographical references and index.

    ISBN 0-7864-1483-9 (softcover : 50# alkaline paper) ∞

    1. School violence—United States—Prevention—Handbooks,
manuals, etc.   2. Education and state—United States.   I. Title.

  LB3013.32.H47   2003
  371.7'82—dc21   2003002511

British Library cataloguing data are available

Manufactured in the United States of America

Cover photograph ©2003 Digital Vision

McFarland & Company, Inc., Publishers
  Box 611, Jefferson, North Carolina 28640
    www.mcfarlandpub.com

Contents

Introduction

This is a book that school principals and central office administrators can use for structuring and restructuring their school safety programs. Its purpose is to provide information about current legislation and groundbreaking initiatives aimed directly at preventing violence in the nation's schools, including Senate bills and state and federal initiatives for improving school safety, discipline and classroom control; model programs and other measures that have proven successful to ensure school safety; strategies for building a successful school safety program; and information about national resource centers, associations, and alliances for safe schools.

School violence ranks next to student and teacher accountability as a major concern of the nation's schools. There is no simple way to achieve the goal of a safe school environment. Much has been done and more needs to be accomplished. No one remedy will work in every school or for every child. Therefore, every effort has been made to provide a variety of strategies and program ideas. Hopefully, a combination of some of these will fit the needs of your school and school district.

Wendy Schwartz, editor of *Preventing Youth Violence in Urban Schools: An Essay Collection*,[1] says that violence among youth is not only one of American society's most pressing concerns, it is also a source of controversy. On the one hand she says, "Youth, like adults, are now more frequently using guns instead of fists to settle disputes. And ... whereas youth violence was once thought to be an urban public school problem and a consequence of poverty and family dysfunction, stable suburban and rural communities are now also experiencing it, as are private schools." On the other hand, she also points out that teachers and administrators who spend their workday in schools think that schools are among "the safest places a child can be." She calls attention to a recent survey, which shows that "the most prevalent type of youth crime is theft, and the most common types of violence are fist fights, bullying, and shoving matches."[2]

Schwartz also says that there are two interesting phenomena concerning attitudes about school violence. The first is the "Ostrich syndrome." Whereas the public generally believes that school violence is ever-present, school leaders are not willing to admit this for fear that the public will boycott communities and schools that are labeled unsafe. Administrators in particular feel that they will be blamed for failing to keep the peace. Gang activity is also ignored as a problem affecting schools and communities "other than this one." Schwartz concludes, "An unfortunate consequence of such denial is that opportunities to reduce violence are lost."[3]

My own experience is consistent with Schwartz's findings. In twenty-seven years working in public schools, at both the school and central office levels, I found that the rule was to not talk about school problems outside the schoolhouse door. Central office staffs, principals, teachers, and support personnel are instructed to keep a tight lip regarding school problems, especially those involving violence, excessive bullying, sexual assaults, and students involved in occult activities. Even the smallest school systems have hired public information officers who are charged with speaking to the press and other public forums, putting the proper spin on problems when they occur.

The second phenomenon Schwartz points out is the contradiction sometimes occurring between school policies and practice. Although most schools and school districts have comprehensive regulations for dealing with violence, she says, "enforcement may be uneven or lax." This has a three-fold effect: students do not feel safe; teachers do not think they are supported in their efforts to prevent violence and impose discipline policies; and the violence-prone believe they will go unpunished. That resource officers have been hired to provide security in middle schools and high school across America should provide some clue as to what is going on inside public school buildings.

William Kilpatrick says, "The core problem facing our schools is a moral one. All the other problems derive from it. Hence, all the various attempts at school reform are unlikely to succeed unless character education is put at the top of the agenda."[4] He continues: "If students don't learn self-discipline and respect for others, they will continue to exploit each other sexually no matter how many health clinics and condom distribution plans are created. If they don't learn habits of courage and justice, curriculums designed to improve their self-esteem won't stop the epidemic of extortion, bullying, and violence; neither will courses designed to make them more sensitive to diversity…. If they don't acquire intellectual virtues such as commitment to learning, objectivity, respect for the truth, and humility in the face of facts, then critical-thinking strategies will only amount to one more gimmick in the curriculum." [5]

As early as 1994, William Bennett, in *The Index of Leading Cultural Indicators: Facts and Figures on the State of American Society,* [6] pointed out that about 3 million thefts and violent crimes occur on or near a school campus each year. This comes to almost 16,000 incidents a day. Bennett also pointed out that 20 percent of high school students now carry a firearm, knife, club, or some other weapon on a regular basis. Character educators have, in general, specified school violence and ineffective parenting as reasons for schools needing programs that enhance the character (civility) of young people. Dr. Philip F. Vincent, in the second edition of his *Rules and Procedures for Character Education, The First Step Toward School Civility,* says, "Good habits and character development are founded on obeying rules and practices. Any longtime teacher will tell you that the failure of students to develop respectful social habits and to follow rules and procedures can handicap them in developing their intellectual skills. And any company personnel director will tell you that failure of employees to follow rules and procedures will handicap their success in any career. As the school climate of caring and civility grows, a safe and orderly environment should evolve, and academic achievement will arise."[7]

About this claim, B. Edward McClellan, writing in *Moral Education in America,* says that by the late 1980s, the character education curriculum developed by the American Institute of Character Education (AICE) in San Antonio, Texas, had reached as many as 18,000 classrooms in 44 states. McClellan explains, "Its effectiveness has been a matter of dispute. Supporters have claimed that it has reduced alcohol and drug abuse, encouraged school attendance, and helped combat vandalism. Skeptics have wondered whether any program that occupied only a few minutes of the school day could have had a substantial impact."[8] He makes clear that the curriculum has provided elementary school materials on moral education, but discloses, "At the same time, it is questionable whether the materials are extensive enough to restore moral education to a central place in the life of the school."[9]

But we should not write off character education just yet. With the new national interest on accountability and its surrogate, the unrelenting testing of students from kindergarten through high school, there has been little time for character education. For that matter, under the aegis of "what gets tested gets taught," the public school curriculum has significantly been narrowed so that even traditional subjects such as social studies, health and physical education, foreign languages, and the arts have been given a secondary status. In many schools, either the number of hours spent in these culture-building and socialization subjects has been reduced (usually unofficially at the school level to gain more time in subjects that are tested) or the subjects have been eliminated from the curriculum altogether. For example, in many elementary schools foreign language has been eliminated from the curriculum for so-called budgetary reasons, but with the understanding that when the budget funding is regained the principal is under no obligation to reinstate the subject, providing more time for memorization and drill in mathematics, science, and language arts.

Four years ago, Jesse Register, then the new superintendent Hamilton County Schools (Chattanooga, Tennessee), met with several leading citizens and discussed the role of education in the life of the community. He pointed out the two major goals of education: to help children become smarter and to help them become better. He suggested the second goal could be achieved through a focus on character education. Representatives of two Chattanooga foundations, the Benwood and Maclellan foundations, helped the school system fund a character education initiative that would foster a moral renewal in the community. It would, they decided, start from the schools and spread out to the community, and then reverse itself, coming from the community back to the schools. Now, four years after making their vision a reality, Chattanooga has been recognized throughout the United States for its remarkable achievements.[10]

A Gift of Character: The Chattanooga Story and *Operating Manual for Character Education Programs* take what has been learned from the Chattanooga experience to help other school systems put together their own character education programs. Dr. Philip F. Vincent, a national leader in character education, was instrumental in helping Chattanooga design their program and train their personnel. I talked with Dr. Vincent about the positive results of the program and this is what he had to say: "They are gathering data. One thing we noticed was a lack of decrease in suspensions. However, on further examination, what we found was a willingness to suspend students for violations that previously were ignored—dress code violations, cussing at teachers, pushing, fights. So what we concluded was that the standards of acceptable behavior continue to be tightened and the majority of students as well as the parents support the policy. We also found that the number of students in the alternative school dropped and more of the students who were sent to the alternative school requested not to leave. It is a climate that models and focuses on civility and service to others within the school. It is a most interesting school that now has students wanting to go there. What is interesting is the high standard of civility that is exhibited there—I think it has something to do with the size of the school and the teachers—go figure!"

Needless to say, character educators, appalled by the growing "amorality" of the school, have blamed the school for the soaring rates of social pathology among youth. They also have pointed to the alarming rates of teenage suicide, crime, drug use, and unwed pregnancies and have called for a renewed commitment to moral education. McClellan says, "The school, they charged, had done much to encourage toleration and to enhance the rights of minorities, but it had said little or nothing about 'individual ethical responsibilities—why we should not murder, rape, assault, or rob our fellow citizens.' If schools failed to provide more guidance, they worried, children would look 'for group values elsewhere, in the sentimental and violent world of television or in the tumultuous and ethically confused world of their peers.'"[11]

Amid the strong tide of accountability and standardized testing, much is being done, and much more is needed, to turn the current of youth violence toward a culture of civility. Perhaps the information and ideas presented here will assist your efforts in that direction.

1

The State of Youth Violence and Its Roots

When we think of aggression and violence, most of us probably think first of crimes committed by one individual against another. Over twenty years ago, when the 1980s began, the United States was experiencing over 20,000 murders per year, over 75,000 rapes, and over 600,000 assaults—in reported crimes alone. Today, those figures are largely unchanged. In addition to these, each year a number of married persons engage in some act of physical violence against their mate, ranging from throwing an object at the other to using a knife or gun on the other. About 2 million Americans have at one time or another beaten up their spouses and another 1.7 million have used a knife or gun on their mates.[1]

According to Straus, Gelles, and Steinmetz,[2] a great many parents commit surprising levels of violence against their own children. Parents physically injure an estimated 1.5 million children each year. Within families, the most violence occurs between siblings, either hitting the other with an object or beating up the other sibling. Because people frequently treat each other so badly, even destructively, social psychologists have tried to understand the causes and results of the violence people do to each other. Their research falls under the general heading of "research on aggression."

On April 21, 1999, the Center for Disease Control's (CDC) National Center for Injury Prevention and Control (NCIPC) reported that it has been working with the federal agencies and other partners in response to the President's charge to collectively come up with the solutions to youth and school violence.[3] In addition, CDC's National

Center for Chronic Disease Prevention and Health Promotion studies youth violence on an ongoing basis. CDC, the U.S. Department of Education, Department of Justice, and the National School Safety Center have examined homicides and suicides associated with schools and identified common features of school-related violent deaths. Their research examines events occurring to and from school, as well as on both public or private school property, or while someone is on the way to an official school-sponsored event. The original CDC cooperative study, published in 1996, yielded these findings:

- Less than 1 percent of all homicides among school-aged children (5–19 years of age) occur in or around school grounds or on the way to and from school.
- 65 percent of school-associated violent deaths were students; 11 percent were teachers or other staff members; and 23 percent were community members who were killed on school property.
- 83 percent of school homicide or suicide victims were males.
- 28 percent of the fatal injuries happened inside the school building; 36 percent occurred outdoors on school property; and 35 percent occurred off campus.
- The deaths included in this study occurred in 25 states across the country and happened in both primary and secondary schools and communities of all sizes.

The report concluded, "Our society demands that schools be safe for our children, yet recent violent events indicate we need to redouble our efforts to prevent violence in schools at the same time we address violence in the larger community."

As of 1999, study results by the CDC show that there were 173 incidents between July 1, 1994, and June 30, 1998. The majority of these incidents were homicides and involved the use of firearms. The total number of events has decreased steadily since the 1992–1993 school year. However, the total number of multiple victim events appears to have increased. During the three school years from August 1995 through June 1998, there were an average of five multiple victim events per year. This is compared to an average of one multiple victim event per year in the three years from August 1992 through July

1995. The report explains, "Thus, while the total number of events of school associated violent deaths has decreased, the total number of multiple-victim events appears to have increased. Data collection ended with the completion of the 1997–1998 academic year."

The CDC's 1997 Youth Risk Behavior Survey (YRBS) reported that:

- 8.3 percent of high school students carried a weapon (e.g., gun, knife, or club) during the 30 days preceding the survey, down from 26.1 percent in 1993.
- 5.9 percent of high school students carried a gun during the 30 days preceding the survey.
- 7.4 percent of high school students were threatened or injured with a weapon on school property during the 12 months preceding the survey.

Other facts from the 1997 YRBS report included:

- Nationwide, 4 percent of students had missed 1 or more days of school during the 30 days preceding the survey because they had felt unsafe at school or when traveling to or from school.
- Overall, male students (12.5 percent) were significantly more likely than female students (3.7 percent) to have carried a weapon on school property.
- Overall, male students (10.2 percent) were significantly more likely than female students (4 percent) to have been threatened or injured with a weapon on school property.
- Nationwide, 14.8 percent of students had been in a physical fight on school property one or more times during the 12 months preceding the survey. Overall, male students (20 percent) were significantly more likely than female students (8.6 percent) to have been in a physical fight on school property. The significant difference was identified for white and Hispanic students and all grade subgroups.
- Approximately one third (32.9 percent) of students nationwide had property (car, clothing, or books) stolen or deliberately damaged on school property one or more times during the 12 months preceding the survey.

CDC's School Health Policies and Programs Study (SHPPS) provides information about school health policies, including violence prevention. The 1994 SHPPS showed that among all school districts, 91 percent have a written policy prohibiting student violence and 80.3 percent have a policy that specifically addresses weapon possession and use among students.

Also, CDC is conducting research to prevent both youth violence and firearm-related violence. As an example, CDC has been studying how to determine which interventions work to prevent violence among youth, both in schools and in the community. CDC will consolidate these evaluation projects on the prevention of youth violence and provide it to programs throughout the U.S. to show what works to prevent youth violence. Preliminary findings include the following:

- Baseline surveys confirm that violent behavior is a problem for young people. For example, four projects reported that 10 percent of participants had recently carried a gun. Moreover, there was a general concern about exposure to violence in schools and neighborhoods.
- The full involvement of the community is critical to developing a sense of ownership for the problem of violence and its solutions.
- The projects found that effective strategies include school-based curricula that emphasize the development of problem solving skills, anger management, and other strategies that help kids develop social skills. In addition, parenting programs that promote strong bonding between parents and children and that teach parents skills in managing conflict in the family, as well as mentoring programs for young people, are also very promising.

The United States
Surgeon General's Report

Donna E. Shalala, Secretary of Health and Human Services, introduced a report on youth violence form the Office of the Surgeon General in 1999.[4]

The first, most enduring responsibility of any society is to ensure the health and well-being of its children. It is a responsibility to which multiple programs of the Department of Health and Human Services are dedicated and an arena in which we can claim many remarkable successes in recent years. From new initiatives in child health insurance and Head Start, to innovative approaches to child care, to the investment in medical research that has ameliorated and even eliminated the threat of many once lethal childhood diseases, we have focused directly and constructively on the needs of millions of children. Through programs designed to enhance the strength and resiliency of families and family members across the life span and through our investments in diverse community resources, we are also helping to enhance the lives and enrich the opportunities of millions more of our children.

Although we can take rightful pride in our accomplishments on behalf of U.S. youths, we can and must do more. The world remains a threatening, often dangerous place for children and youths. And in our country today, the greatest threat to the lives of children and adolescents is not disease or starvation or abandonment, but the terrible reality of violence. We certainly do not know all of the factors that have contributed to creating what many citizens—young and old alike—view as our culture of violence. It is clear, however, that as widespread as the propensity for and tolerance of violence is throughout our society—and despite efforts that, since 1994, have achieved dramatic declines in official records of violence on the part of young people—every citizen must assume a measure of responsibility for helping to reduce and prevent youth violence. Information is a powerful tool, and this Surgeon General's report is an authoritative source of information. In directing the Surgeon General to prepare a scholarly report that would summarize what research can tell us about the magnitude, causes, and prevention of youth violence, President Clinton sought a public health perspective on the problem to complement the extraordinary work and achievements in this area that continue to be realized through the efforts of our criminal and juvenile justice systems. Over the past several months, the Department of Health and Human Services has worked with many hundreds of dedicated researchers, analysts, and policy makers whose interests and expertise lie outside the traditional domains of health and human services. What has become clear through our collaboration is that collectively we possess the tools and knowledge needed to throw safety lines to those young Americans who already have been swept up in the currents of violence and to strengthen the protective barriers that exist in the form of family, peers, teachers, and the countless others whose lives are dedicated to the futures of our children.

This Surgeon General's report seeks to focus on action steps that all Americans can take to help address the problem, and continue to build a legacy of health and safety for our young people and the Nation as a whole. Jeffrey P. Koplan, M.D., Director, Centers for Disease Control and Prevention, Joseph H. Autry III, M.D., Acting Administrator, Substance Abuse and Mental Health Services Administration, and Steven E. Hyman, M.D., Director of the National Institute of mental Health for the National Institutes of Health, comment:

> The opportunity for three Federal agencies, each with a distinct public health mission, to collaborate in developing the Surgeon General's report on youth violence has been an invigorating and rewarding intellectual challenge. We and our respective staffs were pleased to find that the importance that we collectively assign to the topic of youth violence transcended any impediments to a true, shared effort. Obstacles that one might have anticipated—for example, difficulties in exchanging data and discussing concepts that emanate from many different scientific disciplines—proved to be surmountable. Indeed, many of the differences in perspective and scientific approach that distinguish the Centers for Disease Control and Prevention (CDC), the National Institutes of Health (NIH), and the Substance Abuse and Mental Health Services Administration (SAMHSA), when combined, afforded us a much fuller appreciation of the problem and much firmer grounds for optimism that the problem can be solved than is obvious from within the boundaries, or confines, of a single organization. The mission of CDC is to promote health and quality of life by preventing and controlling disease, injury, and disability. The NIH, of which the National Institute of Mental Health (NIMH) is one component, is responsible for generating new knowledge that will lead to better health for everyone. SAMHSA is charged with improving the quality and availability of prevention, treatment, and rehabilitation services in order to reduce illness, death, disability, and cost to society resulting from substance abuse and mental illnesses. Common to each of the agencies is an interest in preventing problems before they have a chance to impair the health of individuals, families, communities, or society in its entirety. Toward this end, CDC, NIH/NIMH, and SAMHSA each support major long-term research projects involving nationally representative samples of our Nation's youth. These studies, which are introduced and described in the report that follows, are designed both to monitor the health status of young Americans and to identify factors that can be shown to carry some likelihood of risk for jeopardizing health—information that lends itself to mounting effective interventions. The designation of youth violence as a public health issue complements the more traditional status of the problem as a criminal justice concern. Here again, it has been satisfying for all of us in the public health sector to reach across professional and disciplinary boundaries to our colleagues in law, criminology, and justice and work to meld data that deepen our understanding of the patterns and nature of violence engaged in by young people throughout our country. What has emerged with star-

tling clarity from an exhaustive review of the scientific literature and from analyses of key new data sources is that we as a Nation have made laudable progress in gaining an understanding of the magnitude of the problem. We have made great strides in identifying and quantifying factors that, in particular settings or combinations, increase the probability that violence will occur. And we have developed an array of interventions of well-documented effectiveness in helping young people whose lives are already marked by a propensity for violence as well as in preventing others from viewing violence as a solution to needs, wants, or problems. CDC, NIH/NIMH, and SAMHSA look forward to continuing collaborations, begun during the development of this report, which will extend further the abilities of policy makers, communities, families, and individuals to understand youth violence and how to prevent it.

The Surgeon General of the United States, David Satcher, M.D., says:

The immediate impetus for this Surgeon General's Report on Youth Violence was the Columbine High School tragedy that occurred in Colorado in April 1999, resulting in the deaths of 14 students, including 2 perpetrators, and a teacher. In the aftermath of that shocking event, both the Administration and Congress requested a report summarizing what research has revealed to us about youth violence, its causes, and its prevention.

Our review of the scientific literature supports the main conclusion of this report: that as a Nation, we possess knowledge and have translated that knowledge into programs that are unequivocally effective in preventing much serious youth violence. Lest this conclusion be considered understated or muted, it is important to realize that only a few years ago, substantial numbers of leading experts involved in the study and treatment of youth violence had come to a strikingly different conclusion. Many were convinced then nothing could be done to stem a tide of serious youth violence that had erupted in the early 1980s. During the decade extending from 1983 to 1993, arrests of youths for serious violent offenses surged by 70 percent; more alarmingly, the number of young people who committed a homicide nearly tripled over the course of that deadly decade. In many quarters, dire predictions about trends in youth violence yielded to resignation; elsewhere, fear and concern prompted well-meaning officials and policy makers to grasp at any proposed solutions, often with little, if any, systematic attention to questions of the efficacy or effectiveness of those approaches.

Fortunately, the past two decades have also been distinguished by the sustained efforts of researchers, legislators, and citizens from all walks of life to understand and address the problem of youth violence. One seminal contribution to these efforts was an initiative taken by one of my predecessors, Surgeon General C. Everett Koop, to address violence as a public health issue; that is, to apply the science of public health to the treatment and prevention of violence. As evident throughout this report, that endorsement was key to encouraging multiple Federal, state, local, and private entities to invest wisely and consistently in research on many facets of youth violence and to translate the knowledge gained into an exciting variety of intervention programs.

Although much remains to be learned, we can be heartened by our accomplishments to date. For one, our careful analyses, together with those conducted by components of the justice system, have demonstrated the pervasiveness of youth violence in our society; no community is immune. In light of that evidence, it has been most encouraging to me to see that the citizens with whom I have interacted in hundreds of communities around the Nation want us to find answers that will help all of our youth. There is a powerful consensus that youth violence is, indeed, our Nation's problem, and not merely a problem of the cities, or of the isolated rural regions, or any single segment of our society.

Equally encouraging have been our findings that intervention strategies exist today that can be tailored to the needs of youths at every stage of development, from young childhood to late adolescence. There is no justification for pessimism about reaching young people who already may be involved in serious violence. Another critical bit of information from our analyses of the research literature is that all intervention programs are not equally suited to all children and youths. A strategy that may be effective for one age may be ineffective for older or younger children. Certain hastily adopted and implemented strategies may be ineffective—and even deleterious—for all children and youth.

Understanding that effectiveness varies underscored for us the importance of bridging the gap between science and practice. Only through rigorous research and thorough, repeated evaluations of programs as they operate in the real world will we be assured that we are using our resources wisely.

In presenting this Surgeon General's report, I wish to acknowledge our indebtedness to the many scientists who have persisted in their work in this difficult, often murky area and whose results we have scrutinized and drawn on. We are also immensely grateful to the countless parents, police officers, teachers, juvenile advocates, health and human service workers, and people in every walk of life who recognize the inestimable value of our Nation's youth and the importance of peace, security, and community in their lives.

Excerpts from the Surgeon General's full report will be included in appropriate places throughout this book.

Report from the Urban Institute

A report from the Urban Institute (a nonpartisan economic and social policy research organization) puts a different slant on violence among youth. The report, *Youth Violence: Perception Versus Reality*,[5] concludes, "As public concern grows over juvenile violence, the juvenile court system is increasingly seen as weak and ineffective. Federal and state legislators are under pressure to pass stricter juvenile crime laws, send more youth to adult court, and make the juvenile system more formalized and adversarial." However, in their report they say that the public's concern about youth violence is "based on inaccurate perceptions of who is responsible for violence in America. Specifically, there is confusion over the difference between crime by juveniles and crime by youth, which includes young adults."

They report that "violence is not primarily juvenile: in 1997, 26 percent of the population was under the age of 18. This group constituted 19 percent of total arrests, 17 percent of violent index arrests, 14 percent of arrests for murder, and 35 percent of arrests over property. When these crime rates are contrasted with adult crime rates, some facts remain hidden such as young adults, ages 18–23, are violent at an even higher rate than juveniles. The report says, "The United States has a profound youth violence problem; juvenile violence is only a part of the problem." For example, from 1980 to 1994, juveniles had a 108 percent increase in arrests for murder, whereas adults had a minus 12 percent increase. A closer examination of the data shows that this increase was among juveniles and youth adults, not juveniles alone. The data shows the murder arrest rate peaking from ages 18 to 20, although it did begin to rise at about the age of 13. The report concludes, "The entire increase in murder arrests between 1980 and 1994 was due to growth in arrests among young people, but adults (ages 18–23) and juveniles (ages 13–17) were equally responsible for the increase." The Urban Institute reaches the following conclusion:

Public perceptions of growing juvenile violence have had serious policy implications in the past decade. State and federal policymakers concluded that something was terribly wrong with the nation's juvenile justice system. States de-emphasized the juvenile court's traditional mission of individualized intervention and rehabilitation and moved to embrace the retribution model used in the criminal justice system. In addition, they enacted policies to send thousands of juveniles to adult court. Yet, as research makes clear, the growing rate of serious violence in the United States during the late 1980s and early 1990s was not due to the behavior of juveniles alone. It reflected a more generalized surge in youth violence.

This suggests that current arrangements for dealing with violent young adults are in need of repair, especially now that the adult justice system is responsible for a larger proportion of all violent young people, including thousands of young offenders once defined as juveniles. In order to address the nation's violence problem more fully, the justice system as a whole should be working to create new and effective approaches to intervening with youth in general.

ABC News.com also reported in 1999 that although youth violence has declined, the levels are still too high.[6] Thomas Simon, of the Center for Disease Control, said, "Researchers found a significant reduction in the fighting, weapon carrying, and fighting-related injuries among high school students between 1991 and 1997." The study by federal violence and injury prevention specialists also found significant reductions in the percentage of students reported carrying a gun, being in a fight on school property or carrying a weapon on school property from 1993 to 1997. Researchers from the CDC analyzed national youth risk behavior surveys for the past several years. Their report appears in a special violence and human rights issue of the *Journal of the American Medical Association*. Among the major findings were that the percentage of 9th through 12th graders carrying a weapon such as a gun, knife, or club anytime within the 30 days prior to the survey decreased by 30 percent; that weapon carrying on school property declined by 28 percent; that carrying a gun decreased by 25 percent; physical fighting both on and off school property declined approximately 15 percent, and being injured in a fight decreased by 20 percent.

Researchers cite several factors for the decline, including improvements in economic conditions, the reduction in the unemployment rate and a drop in the crack cocaine epidemic and gang-related violence. They have also seen a decrease in the amount of firearm-related violence associated with the crack cocaine epidemic. Simon said, "In addition to that, I think it's important to recognize the fact that a lot of attention has been focused on the problem of youth violence since the late 1980s, and as a result of this attention, we've seen new partnerships form between schools and community based organizations and families."

Despite the improvement, the level of violence-related behavior remains unacceptably high, researchers say. In 1997, 18 percent of high school students carried a weapon—and 9 percent carried a weapon while in school. Nearly one in every 16 high school students reported carrying a gun sometime during the previous 30 days, and 37 percent participated in physical fighting during the past 12 months. And not all behaviors associated with violence declined. The percentage of students who reported missing school because they felt unsafe to go and the percentage who reported being threatened or injured with a weapon on school property did not change during the time period studied. This, say the researchers, underscores the need to continue enhancing violence prevention programs.

Defining Aggression

Understanding the psychology of violence (aggression, assault, physical aggression) will greatly aide our efforts in building public school safety programs. We begin by defining "aggression." Social psychologists tell us, "Aggression is any behavior that intentionally hurts others."[7] Including "intentions" in this definition allows us to conclude whether or not an act is intentionally or accidentally aggressive. Intentions seek an explanation or a reason, whereas accidents do not. Sure, we want to discover what caused an accident or if an action is accidental at all. Once we deem a behavior intentional or accidental, then we can ask the appropriate questions to find out more information. We can't ignore "intention" for intention implies purpose and reason. For example, accidentally pushing another person may not be an act of aggressive behavior but intentionally pushing is. In Texas, the action of a mom who drowned her five young children can't be labeled accidental under the circumstances. Neither can it be labeled intentional until the question of sanity is answered. Here is the gray area of moral or amoral behavior. Be that as it may, in normal situations, intention has a central role in our judgments about aggression because it defines the behavior in terms of "trying to cause harm." Intention separates accidents from behaviors designed to cause harm; thus, we are able to judge intentional behaviors as moral or immoral, based on whether they cause or do not cause physical, social, or emotional harm to another person.

Sometimes aggressive actions are good. The question is whether they breach the precepts of a decent society; whether they violate the conditions of human rights and human dignity. If an aggressive act— by a police officer or soldier, for example—is within the bounds of commonly accepted social norms, we can label them "sanctioned aggression." These behaviors normally fall somewhere between anti-social and prosocial behaviors. We may act aggressively in self-defense when attacked by another person, or a teacher or coach may act appropriately by disciplining a disobedient student or player. None of these acts is required of the person, but they fall within the bounds of what is permitted by social norms. They do not violate accepted moral standards.

In his book, *The Decent Society*,[8] Avishai Margalit discusses the foundations of human decency in terms of "humiliation;" that is, in terms of any "sort of behavior or condition that constitutes a sound reason for a person to consider his or her self-respect injured." "Humiliation" is further defined as "a break in a person's ability to be self-sufficient in satisfying his/her needs." Although Margalit focuses more on psychological aggression, via humiliation, his insights are pertinent for this discussion. He observes that only humans can produce humiliation—even without intent. For him a decent society is one that fights conditions of humiliation. A decent society, at all levels—from family and government organizations to churches and schools—develops programs and policies to prevent aggressive behavior by persons, groups, and institutions. Violence by juveniles or adults is unacceptable. Violence violates the canons of decency, the precepts of morality, and the social codes of civility.

We can make another distinction, between aggressive behavior and aggressive feelings, such as anger. A person may be quite angry inside, but make no overt effort to hurt another person. Society civility can only exist when individuals control their aggressive feelings most of the time. Society places strong restraints on acts of violence, and most individuals, even those who feel angry much of the time, rarely act aggressively. This turns our attention back to ethics and a reasoned concern for human behavior and its outcomes. According to

Philip Selznick, the general consequences of morality are "human well-being" and "the general good."[9] Moral well being is more that sympathy and concern. It entails a kind of will or commitment and competence, which requires reflection as well as feeling, and responsibility as well as love. For John Dewey, it demands an ability to distinguish "the enjoyed and the enjoyable, the desired and the desirable, the satisfying and the satisfactory."[10] Moral competence is character defining, a variable attribute of persons, communities, and institutions who call themselves "civil." Within character, the task of moral awareness is to replace uncontrolled and unreflective behavior with more controlled and deliberate ways of developing oneself. As Selznick says, "The question is: What kind of person, institution, or community will result from following a particular course of conduct or from adopting a given rule or policy? This focuses attention on the internal relevance of what we do; and it allows the conclusion that consequences for character will have priority, in many important cases, over consequences for particular ends such as winning a game or managing an enterprise."[11]

The Sources of Anger

This internal feeling of aggression is called "anger." There is no one alive who has not experienced anger; indeed, most of us have felt like hurting someone else sometimes in our lives. Most people say they feel at least mildly or moderately angry anywhere from several times a day to several times a week. Of course, most anger is not expressed openly. Although anger cannot be observed directly, psychologists and social psychologists report a considerable amount of research on the factors that arouse anger. They report three primary sources of anger, from which the relationship to aggression may be defined causally (cause-effect or stimulus-response) or by reason. Although anger may come on suddenly, its aggressive response may be delayed, thought about, and then acted upon as a "reasoned" response to the situation.

Being Attacked by Another Person. One of the most common sources of anger is being attacked or bothered by someone, either physically or by being humiliated and frustrated. When students are made to feel stupid in class or by their parents, they tend to get angry and act aggressively toward the source of their anger. The tendency of people, when attacked, is to respond with retaliation. Retaliation may come immediately as an effect of the person's anger or some time later as a thought-out and calculated response. One of the consequences of retaliation within families is domestic violence, which breeds additional violence.

Frustration. Frustration occurs when we are blocked from achieving the attainment of a goal or when we are denied the things we most want. Social psychologists respond that frustration tends to arouse feelings of aggression. Barker, Dembo, and Lewin provided the classic example of frustration in 1941.[12] Their experiment involved children who were shown a room full of toys but were not allowed to enter it. They stood outside looking at the toys, wanting to play with them, but were unable to reach them. In time they were granted permission to enter the room and play with the toys. Other children were given the toys without first being prevented from playing with them. The children who had been frustrated smashed the toys on the floor, threw them against the wall, and behaved very destructively. The children who had not been frustrated were much quieter and less destructive.

In the broader society, economic depression can bring on frustration. People cannot find jobs or buy the things they or their families want and need. All phases of their lives are restricted: people are downsized, departments are collapsed, there are lateral moves, and those once in positions of authority are moved further down the ladder, reducing their status in the workplace and, sometimes their salaries; others are laid-off permanently, while those at the top retain their positions and are often rewarded financially for "saving" the company. The consequence is that frustration increases and various forms of aggression become more common. Howland and Sears (1940)[13] and Mintz (1946)[14] provided evidence for increased aggressive behavior during economic hard times. They found a strong relationship between the price of cotton and the number of blacks lynched in the South during the years 1882 and 1930. When cotton prices were high, lynchings were down; but when cotton prices were low, the number of lynchings was relatively high. This has an indirect relationship to juvenile violence and school safety. As family violence increases, the propensity of juveniles to engage in aggressive and sometimes violent behaviors also proliferates. Aggression begets aggression.

Family violence is the most commonly reported source of conflict in America.[15] Mostly, families argue and fight over housekeeping: about what and how much to clean, the quality of food served, taking out the trash, mowing the lawn, and fixing things that are broken. One-third of American couples say they always disagree about housekeeping duties. Close behind are conflicts about sex, social activities, money, and children. The consequence of frustration is always aggression. According to Dollard and Doob,[16] the occurrence of aggressive behavior *nearly* always presupposes the existence of frustration and, contrariwise, the existence of frustration *nearly* always leads to some form of aggression. There are, of course, factors other than frustration that can produce aggressive behavior.

Getting Really Mad. For an event to produce excessive anger and aggressive behavior, for a person to get really mad, that person must recognize that the attack is intended to harm.[17] If a victim acknowledges that the frustration was caused by unavoidable circumstances, then not much anger will be created. But, if there are no *justifying external forces*, the anger is much greater. If a victim perceives an action as voluntary and unjustified, there is usually more anger. Normally, arbitrary and unjustified actions that frustrate produce more anger and aggressive behavior. When this happens to one of us, we just want to know "why" the person attacked, either physically or with words. A usual response is, "What did I do to deserve this?"

Freud, McDougall, and Lorenz have said that humans have an innate drive to fight.[18] They argued that just as human beings have feelings of hunger, thirst, or sexual arousal, they have an innate need to behave aggressively. They argue that even though there are no known psychological mechanisms connected with aggressive feelings, aggression is a basic drive. On the other hand, this definition of aggression as requiring the intent to harm may not be appropriate for much of this behavior. Sears et al. argue, "Although some continue to be convinced that all animals have instinctive aggressive drives, most psychologists now dispute this. Among animals relatively low on the phylogenetic scale, instinct plays an important role in producing aggression, but there seems little reason to believe that humans have instinctive impulses toward aggressiveness."[19]

In his studies on anger and aggression, J. R. Averill[20] defines how people respond when they feel angry under four basic response types:

1. Direct aggression
   Verbal or symbolic aggression
   Denial or removal of some benefit
   Physical aggression or punishment
2. Indirect aggression
   Telling a third party in order to get back at the instigator
   Harming something important to the instigator
3. Displaced aggression
   Against a nonhuman object
   Against a person
4. Non-aggressive responses
   Engaging in calming activities
   Talking the incident over with a neutral party; no intent to harm the offender
   Talking the incident over with the offender without exhibiting hostility
   Engaging in activities opposite to the instigation of anger

Learning Aggression

Being attacked by another person or being frustrated by unattained goals make people feel angry and these feelings of anger often lead to some kind of aggressive behavior. But some people are angered or frustrated and never behave aggressively. This leads to the premise that the main force behind human aggression is past learning. Experiences in society are our greatest teacher and there are four learned social influences that can produce aggressive behavior.[21] These are reinforcement, imitation, social norms, and individual differences.

Reinforcement. When a person is rewarded for a particular behavior, the person is more likely to repeat that behavior in the future. When the person is punished, he or she is less likely to repeat it. When a child is punished for fighting, biting his mother, or generally misbehaving in school, he or she learns not to do these things. The child is rewarded when he or she restrains himself or herself despite frustrations and this is learned also. Aggressive acts are, to a major extent, learned responses, and parents and teachers can reinforce them, unknowingly, when they go unpunished.

Imitation. All human beings, particularly children, have a strong propensity to imitate others. We learn by watching and we learn to learn by watching and listening. Children listen with their minds as well as with their ears. They also listen with their emotions and many times respond emotionally to aggression and frustration. When a child observes others being aggressive or controlling their aggression, behavior is being influenced, substantiated, and sometimes changed. The child learns verbal aggression as they experience it from their parents and peers. The child learns non-aggressive behaviors as well.

Another skill that is learned is when aggression is or is not permissible. Children do not imitate indiscriminately; they imitate some people more than others. Watching a child's basketball game is a study in contrast. The meek young girls and boys will imitate the more agile and aggressive players because they are successful in scoring baskets, dribbling the ball, and defending others. The more important, powerful, and successful people are the more they will be imitated by others. Children have a tendency to imitate those whom they see more often, including their parents, the primary models for a child's behavior during the early years. So do their more aggressive peers. Psychologists report that "Since parents are both the major source of reinforcement and the chief object of imitation, a child's future aggressive behavior depends greatly on how parents treat the child and on how they themselves behave."[22]

Although punished for aggressive behavior at home, the child's aggression may continue outside the home where the threat of punishment is the weakest. The child is actually imitating the parent's aggressive behavior. When children are in a situation where they have the upper hand, they act the way their parents do toward them. If parents are aggressive, their children will more than likely be aggressive as well. Punishment teaches the child to select wisely where his or her aggression can be displayed without rousing the attention of an adult such as a parent or teacher. Children who learn aggression at home also learn that aggression is acceptable if they can get away with it. Regardless of what parents teach, children will continue to do what their parents do, as well as what they say.

Another way of looking at families is to observe the amount of violence that occurs in what is supposed to be a refuge from the harsh outside world. The extensiveness of family violence suggests that violence is normal in normal families. Research shows that violence is more likely to occur at the hands of a family member than it is at the hands of anyone else. Even though the world outside the family is less violent than the world inside the family, paradoxically, the loving and supporting aspects of the family obscure our ability to perceive and understand its violent aspects and discourage any attempt at facing up to how much violence is there. Educators can never overestimate the influence of parents on a child's behavior. Children are constantly becoming their parents, reacting to or acting out the violence they receive at home.

Social Norms. Socialization is a lifelong process of learning the ways of society. This process takes place in group settings, first in the family, then in play groups, followed by more formal group associations in the institutions of education and religion, and as adults in economic and political institutions. As we grow, so do our contacts and roles within our expanding group. Most of our interactions with others take place in groups.

Normally, we learn the general norms (rules of behavior) of our society that regulate when and where it is appropriate to use aggressive behavior. Children are permitted to scream and yell during ballgames, at opposing players or even referees, but in the classroom they are not permitted to yell at each other or at the teacher. We also learn whether or not to aggress as a habitual response to certain cues, such as being hit by another person. If such aggression-eliciting cues are present, anger is more likely to be converted into aggression. But if aggression-suppressing cues are evident, anger is not likely to turn into aggressive behavior. A major question for educators is, are parents and teachers teaching their children and students how to control or suppress their violent tendencies when they are angered or frustrated?

One purpose of social norms is to fine-tune aggression-eliciting and aggression-suppressing cues.[23] Again, these are learned behaviors. We learn from our society the norms governing *prosocial aggression* where aggression is the appropriate behavior; *sanctioned aggression*— the situations where aggression is permitted, but not required, such as self-defense; and we also learn what is thought to be *anti-social aggression*, such as murder and assault, which is not permitted by society. When these are not learned, children are apt to use aggressive behavior as their first response to anger and frustration, maltreatment and humiliation. When children use aggression most of the time as their initial reaction to others, counseling and re-socialization are needed to re-orient the child to social norms.

Individual Differences. Social psychologists have found that some individuals are much more aggressive than others.[24] Some are bullies and violent criminals, while others are gentle and law-abiding. Men are generally more physically aggressive than women, though research is less clear about verbal aggression. People from lower class backgrounds have been found to be more aggressive than those from middle class backgrounds. In longitudinal studies, which measured aggression at age 8 and then at age 30, there was a significant relationship among a variety of indicators of aggression such as spouse abuse, criminal convictions, drunk driving, and self-rated aggressiveness. The most aggressive children were most likely to be the most aggressive adults later on.

Normally, learning social norms consistently regulates the behavior of individuals. The exception to this is mob or crowd behavior. People in crowds often feel free to gratify savage, destructive instincts. Within crowds they feel invincible and anonymous. This phenomenon is called *deindividuation*,[25] which often entails unrestrained and aggressive behavior. One form of imitative aggression that is significant in school violence and crowd behavior is *contagious violence*. Teenagers seem to be particularly susceptible to contagious violence, especially in large groups at ball games, in the cafeteria, restrooms, or in hallways. Contagious violence is most evident in group situations. It can result in mob fights, bottle throwing, the use of weapons, and more.

Reducing Aggressive Behavior

Aggressive behavior is a major problem for human societies and can be found in every institution, household, public forum, and school. Large-scale social violence and individual crimes are extremely damaging and harmful to the general social fabric. Within the schoolhouse, a great deal of time, money, and energy is being spent simply to control the human tendency toward violence. It is vital that educators and parents understand how to reduce and control aggressiveness.

Researchers tell us that three factors determine the extent of aggressiveness in particular situations[26]: (1) the strength of the person's angry feelings, which are determined by the degree of frustration and the person's interpretation of this frustration that produced them; (2) the tendency to express anger, which is determined by what the person has learned about aggression in general and by the nature of the situation in particular; and (3) the instrumental reasons for committing violence. Instrumental aggression is "aggression used to attain some practical goal by hurting others." People kill for reasons other than anger and frustration. They may be paid to murder or hurt someone else. Sometimes a criminal will hurt someone in order to steal his or her possessions. Hurting others is a way of attaining valued goods, but not because of angry feelings. This analysis indicates to us some of the ways in which aggressive behavior can be reduced. For example, frustration can be reduced, people can be taught not to aggress in some particular situations, and they can be taught to restrain aggressiveness in general. There are some techniques for reducing aggressive behavior. These include the following.

Punishment and Retaliation. Obviously, fear of punishment or retaliation should suppress some aggressive behavior. Rational individuals will examine the future consequences of their aggressive behavior and will avoid behaving aggressively if punishment seems likely. This also tells us that younger children are more likely to be victims of domestic violence than older children, for they are unable to retaliate. Also, children who are frequently punished for being aggressive turn out themselves to be more aggressive than normal because they model themselves on the aggression they have received. Frequent punishment is like being attacked: it generates a lot of anger and frustration. It does not automatically inhibit the aggression of children.

If a child (or any person for that matter) lives in constant fear of punishment or retaliation, *counteraggression*[27] seems to be the result. People who are attacked have a tendency to retaliate against their attackers, even when this retaliation will surely bring more attacks. Retaliation is commonplace in schools. Schools, like society in general, have too many people in too many places for all to be monitored constantly. Therefore, it is simply impossible to depend on external controls to minimize violence. Because aggression breeds additional aggression, the thought of retaliation is not a general solution to the problem of violence.

Reducing Frustration. Reducing frustration is a better technique for reducing aggression. Experts say that any effort to reduce instrumental aggression must focus on the underlying causes of aggression as well as the overt behavior itself. We avoid violence by teaching children to inhibit their aggressive impulses, by trying to make them less angry, or by threatening them with retaliation. We also can avoid violence by patient and diplomatic efforts to reduce real conflicts. There will always be conflict between parents and children, or between co-workers or schoolmates; no one will ever have exactly what and as much as he or she wants; some people will never be able to achieve what they would like; some will always be dissatisfied with what their friends do; and the list never ends. The best we can do is to examine the causes of frustration and try to eliminate as much of it as possible. Because all frustration will never be entirely eliminated, we must turn to other techniques for minimizing violence.

Learned Inhibitions. A major way to reduce aggression and violent behavior is to teach children (and adults) how to control their own aggressive behavior. Children must learn when aggression should and must be suppressed. They need to learn how to suppress their aggressive behavior in general and how to suppress it in specific situations. If possible, children need to be taught to recognize their personal aggression anxiety. Not everyone has equal amounts of aggression anxiety: women tend to have more than men, and children reared in middle class homes have more than children reared in lower class homes. Parents who use reasoning and withdrawal of affection as disciplinary techniques produce children with more aggression anxiety than parents who use high degrees of physical punishment. Aggression anxiety is our internal warning system, a red flag that anger and frustration are mounting. Without it, we are more apt to lash out at others when provoked and, sometimes, without warning.

Children can also learn to recognize their own anxiety and growing aggression in certain specific situations. They can learn how to express their anxiety non-violently, which will also reduce their frustration and lessen the chance of reacting violently toward another child. Children and adults learn constantly—all through our lives we are learning and relearning the norms of our social environments. Psychologists tell us that we all possess a great many keenly categorized distinctions about what is and what is not permissible aggression.[28] For example, we learn that it is okay to yell at children but that it is not all right to beat them up; we can kill animals for sport and food, but it's not right to kill someone's pet animal; and we can't curse our teachers to their faces and teachers can't throw things at their students. Our learned inhibitions represent the most potent controls of human violent behavior we have. There are not enough government authorities to catch every crime and every aggressive act; we must learn to control ourselves.

Self-Control. In my 1995 book, *Bridges: Building Relationships and Resolving Conflicts,*[29] the idea of "rationality as self-control" was developed from the writings of John Dewey and Charles Sanders Peirce. The following themes capture the essence of this concept:

1. Education is a continuous process of reconstruction in which there is a progressive movement away from the child's immature experience to experience that becomes more pregnant with meaning, more systematic and controlled.

2. The goal of education is the development of creative intelligence, which consists of a complex set of flexible and growing habits that involve sensitivity, the ability to understand the complexities of situations, imagination that is exercised in seeing new possibilities, fairness and objectivity in judging and evaluating conflicting values and opinions, and the courage to change one's views when it is demanded by the consequences of our actions and the criticism of others.

3. The image of human behavior that emerges from this point of view is that we are "craftsmen," active manipulators advancing our own ideas, actively testing them, always open to ongoing criticism, and reconstructing ourselves and our environment. As Dewey noted, the development of selfhood is an active process.

The basic theme of *Bridges*, which began as a book in character education and ended as a general treatise on human relations and conflict resolution, is that we should make an effort to build an ethical relationship between our reasoning abilities, our conduct, and the development of our characters. In essence, "The dynamics of conflict and cooperation, and the movement to resolve conflict in the direction of a cooperative society, are essential elements in this process." The goal of human societies in general, and of school safety programs in particular, is that we should act rationally and identify with each other in "certain ethical and human ways, ways that are linked to creative growth, openness to experience, and responsibility for behavior." As we work toward this ideal, we will form more stable patterns of cooperation and conflict resolution.

An ethical situation is one where conflict calls for practical judgment, and where selection of a course of action relies on "good" character. Schools need to remember that in institutions and societies where there is no latitude of action and no compromise, where there is always only one permissible strategy, behavior becomes ritualized and rational power disappears. When children are not given flexibility and space to laugh, talk, joke, and intermingle with their friends without being smothered by supervising adults, they will display aggressive and negative behaviors. Increasing self-control requires rationality, openness and fairness, a method of weighing alternatives, evaluating options, and assessing obligations.

If the goal of school safety programs is to educate students for creative intelligence and self-control, then our efforts must be educational as well as rule bearing. We must teach them to reconsider their personal and very complex habits and values. We sincerely hope they will develop patterns of behavior that include sensitivity to others and the school and family environments; the ability to discern the complexities of situations; imagination exercised in seeing new possibilities for behavior; a willingness to learn from experience; fairness and objectivity exercised in judging and evaluating conflicting values and opinions; and the courage to change their views according to the consequences of their actions.

2

Public School Safety:
Government Initiatives

To deal specifically with violence in schools, President Bill Clinton signed the 1994 Gun-Free Schools Act, mandating a one-year expulsion for students who bring weapons to school and bolstering the "zero tolerance" for weapons policies already existing in some states and school districts. Also, the Federal government, and most states, make funds available for prevention activities through anti-crime and education legislation. These include anti-gang programs and other violence-focused prevention education, as well as more general recreational activities.

Legislation now exists at all levels of government to reduce the availability of guns, particularly the sale of weapons to minors. Weapons offenses are adjudicated more harshly in general, and the practice of trying violent juvenile offenders as adults is growing. Some states now hold parents legally responsible for certain behaviors of their children, such as truancy and delinquency.

This chapter will review these legislative efforts and more. Information is gathered from government reports and initiatives, government resources that offer guidelines and support in the general area of public school safety, and the priorities of the U. S. Department of Education. Although not its primary intention, this chapter will also provide a sampling of pertinent state initiatives and laws on school discipline, drug abuse, and school safety.

Today, the old ways of teaching and school organization are gradually giving way to new ways that reflect the crisis of public school safety. In the early 1980s, business and industry were turning away from the command, measure, and control model of management—a 19th century workplace model developed by Frederick Taylor in 1881 for the purpose of standardizing and controlling industrial production.[1] This model was later adopted by public schools for sorting and selecting students for placement in college or the industrial complex as either workers or managers. Standardized curricula and testing, teacher performance criteria, and the carrot of higher pay reinforced it for those who delivered a better product. Teachers still complain that they could deliver a better product if they only had better raw materials. Students are still thought of as a commodity. The 19th century is still with us.

But from about 1960, the world of public education, as the society in general, began to change from being product-oriented to being information and service-oriented. Prior to 1960, the purpose of transportation was to move people; since then, it has been to move information. Schools, businesses, and industries have been, or are being, wired in order to connect them to the global bank of electronic information. More and more, information that was once available to only a few is being transferred to an electronic base, which is accessible to all who have an internet hookup.

Today, knowledge workers are being employed in great numbers. Success is not thought of as achieving by doing what one knows how to do, but rather of achieving by risking failure. The modern day winter Olympics provides a clear metaphor of these changes—snowboarding, figure skating, and the aerials witnessed in acrobatic ski jumping broke with standardized and traditional maneuvers to include actions never witnessed before in the Olympics. Sometimes the judges seemed not to know how to rate these athletes. Their achievements, although highlighted by the media, seemed to lie somewhere outside the box of normal scoring by the Olympic judges.

As innovation and creativity have become important values in the workplace and in athletics, they have been de-emphasized in schools. Peter Drucker reminds his readers that if we do things the way they have always been done, we will get what we have always gotten.[2] What is standard fare today, because of innovation and creative leadership, will be outdated in just a few years. Drucker recommends *participatory leadership* based on a calculus of potential rather than one of probability as a general model for business and industry, and this model can also be effective in schools. This model will lie outside the causal chains of modern scientific thought with its command-measure-control mentality. It assumes a connection with other information sources, many of which are electronic.

This means that more will be involved in pubic school safety programs than standardized school construction, standardized teaching models, and standardized models of student evaluation and discipline. The problem is more complex than that. Much more is involved in the education of a child and part of the calculus of potential involves both the teachers' and the students' creativity, insights, and innovations. Public school safety programs will necessitate involvement by all significant community and government agencies, parents, churches, teachers, students themselves, and citizen volunteers. The foundation of such programs is participatory leadership. There is no one and no organization that goes unaffected by public school and juvenile violent activities.

Phillip C. Selechty believes that schools need to be reinvented with this vision in mind.[3] Attitudes and vision will be essential parts of the public school safety model as they change the environment of the school. Selechty says we should acknowledge, as we approach the task of developing public school safety programs, that effective leadership is driven by one's character, which includes motivation, purpose, beliefs, and values. These basic ingredients empower us to embrace new goals and workplace practices. It makes no sense to initiate character education programs for students if the character of the community and the school environment is left untouched.

There are many keys to developing public school safety programs. Perhaps the first is to realize that schools are in transition and mirror the general changes in society. Therefore, the school environment must reflect a clear vision emanating from the core values and beliefs of its administrators, teachers, parents, and students. Consensus must be found among those who live and work in this environment. Actions are then to be aligned with these values. Parents and administrators, community leaders and students must take the lead in fashioning school safety programs. Kevin Cashman challenges us to become "servant-leaders"—to not only provide leadership for safety programs, but to become involved in actualizing—serving—these programs as well.[4] The following "keys" to becoming a servant leader were adapted from *Leadership from the Inside Out* by Cashman:

- Live with integrity and lead by example.
- Develop strategies that focus on student success and self-development.
- Manage change, set priorities, create a vision, and be trustworthy.
- Invite parents and students to share their authority, knowledge, and the responsibility for student success.
- Inspire peers and students to achieve success.
- Respond to plurality within the diverse student community.
- Let student needs and success drive teaching.
- Become result oriented by empowering students with knowledge about how to learn.
- Get students actively engaged in working on and with knowledge.
- Encourage intelligent risk-taking among students and teachers.
- Make decisions that solve rather than create problems.
- Don't be afraid of hard work, for that's what any school safety program will take.

Federal Government Initiatives

School administrators need to know and understand the commitment of the federal government to solving the problem of school aggression and violence. The following timeline provides an overview of government initiatives concerning public school safety since 1996. The initiatives include shared and cooperative projects by several federal departments and single, one-department reports. The specific recommendations of these agencies, although abbreviated here, can be read in full by using the referenced Internet site. The suggestions of these agencies range from developing model programs to providing step-by-step strategies for schools (school systems) to follow. Following this timeline of initiatives will be additional recommendations from state governments, national organizations such as the National Education Association (NEA), relevant federal laws that have been either proposed or passed, and a sampling of relevant state laws focusing on school safety. Because there is much overlapping, the details of these reports will be summarized in chapters two and three—under strategies for building school safety programs and outlines of model programs themselves.

Timeline

September 1996

In preparation for developing an action guide to help schools create school safety programs, the U.S. Department of Justice, in September 1996, nominated the following procedures for creating safe, orderly, and drug-free schools[5]:

- **Placing school safety high on the educational agenda.** Such a priority involves making a personal and community commitment toward creating a safe, welcoming, respectful, gun-free, and drug-free school.
- **Involving parents and citizens.** Planners must make certain to bring parents, school administrators, and community leaders to the table in order to shape strategies and programs together. Those affected by Safe School Plans should be involved throughout the entire process.
- **Building and developing the team.** Making schools safe is a joint responsibility, requiring a broad-based team and a working attitude emphasizing collaboration and cooperation. Team members should include educators, parents, students, law enforcers, community and business leaders, probation and court representatives, social service and health care providers, and other youth-serving professionals.
- **Conducting the school site assessment.** Team members should determine the specific issues and concerns that the local community believes are most important. This step begins the process of developing a meaningful Safe School Plan that will foster an increased level of community commitment.
- **Reviewing the law.** The law is at the heart of every major school safety issue today. Laws are intended to articulate the reasonable standards that define the delicate balance between student rights and student responsibilities. The law proclaims what must be done, implies what should be done, and establishes limits for what may be done. The law constitutes a code of professional expectations for school administrators and youth-serving professionals. As planning begins, school and community leaders should consult with the school district's attorneys to ensure that legal issues are appropriately addressed. Constitutional issues, as well as other concerns ranging from adequate liability insurance to the effective screening of volunteers, may arise with the implementation of a comprehensive violence prevention program.

- **Creating a Safe School Plan.** This is an action plan that not only includes the substance of what is necessary to accomplish, but also identifies the processes by which those goals will be achieved, including short-term objectives and long-term systemic changes. It is most important for team members to understand that they can make a positive difference in the quality of life for themselves, their community, and all the children they serve.
- **Formulating a contingency plan.** Having a backup plan for handling emergencies and crises simply makes good sense. Such foresight can prevent a crisis and preclude successive crises while creating an effective mechanism for managing school problems.
- **Creating an educational climate.** Team members should evaluate the current education atmosphere and propose modifications that will transform it into a safe, vibrant learning environment in which students and teachers respect each other.
- **Searching for ways to serve students and ways students can serve.** Young people should always be included as part of the solution to the problems associated with juvenile delinquency. Actively engaging students in school and community projects and activities creates a level of ownership that supports the success of every child.
- **Getting the message out and communicating.** Working with the media may be one of the most successful strategies for building awareness of both the issues involved and the progress being made. With simple newsletters, schools can share success stories and break down barriers with other districts and schools.
- **Evaluating progress.** It is important to monitor activities, measure impact, and evaluate how the plan is working. A Safe School Plan should be modified and improved whenever necessary.

These guidelines represent the beginning of a continuing team process to create safe schools for all of America's children. Making schools safe requires a total community effort within the context of a broad spectrum of opportunities. There are no simple solutions. Each school and each school district has its own unique challenges and its own resources. The *Action Guide* developed by the Department of Justice can be read in its entirety using the Internet site referenced in endnote 5. These action steps will be outlined in Chapter 3—"Strategies for Building a School Safety Program"—along with other pertinent recommendations from other agencies.

July 1997

Consistent with the vision of strong, safe and academically sound schools, the U.S. Department of Education issued seven educational priorities. The seventh of these stated, "Every School Will Be Strong, Safe, Drug-Free and Disciplined."[6] The Department of Education said that Priority Seven is indeed important because "children cannot learn to high standards in schools that are overwhelmed by violence, drug use or facilities in disrepair." Priority seven aims to ensure strong and healthy school environments where children can learn best and achieve to their potential. School environment encompasses the culture of the school, the physical surroundings of the school, and the school's health and safety.

Essential pillars of strong and healthy learning environments include the following: (1) schools that are structurally sound and conducive to learning; (2) schools that are safe, orderly, and free from drugs; and, (3) public school choice which allows parents to choose the best school for their children based on their individual differences. Respecting individual student differences and recognizing their varying strengths, interests and learning styles, in fact, is a central element of a positive environment.

June 15, 1998

Senator Stewart Greenleaf, R-Montgomery, with the assistance of PSEA (Public Safety Executive Association) President David J. Gondak, submitted legislation that is in line with many of the recommendations of PSEA's 1994 Task Force on Violent and Disruptive Students and Change That Works, the association's education reform agenda.[7]

The legislation will:

- Expand "in loco parentis" to all school employees who have charge of students (currently limited to professional teachers and principals).
- Require conflict resolution training for teachers and instruction for students.
- Provide for maintenance of disciplinary actions when a student transfers.
- Provide civil and criminal immunity for school employees who assist injured students (Good Samaritan).
- Require reporting by school employees acting on reasonable suspicion of a criminal act of violence or a potential criminal act of violence.
- Allow districts to maintain a civil action against parents or guardians for property damage by students, with a community service alternative provided for those who cannot pay.

- Provide disciplinary and counseling procedures for drug and alcohol violations.
- Provide procedures for placement of violent or disruptive special education students in alternative education settings.
- Establish a pilot program for six schools with expanded alternative education.
- Allow for consideration of alternative education placement based on a student's delinquency status in the determination of safety risks posed by the student.
- Provide for enhanced criminal penalties for school-related assaults and terroristic threats.

1998–2002

The Office of the Surgeon General, prior to the election of President George W. Bush, issued detailed information and statistics about youth and public school violence.[8] Under the Surgeon General's guidance, these agencies established a Planning Board comprising individuals with expertise in diverse disciplines and professions involved in the study, treatment, and prevention of youth violence. The Planning Board also enlisted individuals representing various Federal departments, including particularly the Department of Justice (juvenile crime aspects of youth violence), the Department of Education (school safety issues), and the Department of Labor (the association between youth violence and youth employment, and out-of-school youth). Invaluable assistance was obtained as well from individual citizens who have founded and operate nonprofit organizations designed to meet the needs of troubled and violent youths. Most important, young people themselves accepted invitations to become involved in the effort. All of these persons helped to plan the report and participated in its prepublication reviews.

The complete report from the Surgeon General's office is book-length. It can be downloaded from the site referenced in endnote 8. Appropriate parts of this report will be synthesized and presented with the recommendations from other agencies in Chapters 3 and 4.

October 1999

In October 1999, the White House issued the following a press release which read in part[9]: "Today the President will also announce that the Justice Department—in partnership with MTV and the

Department of Education—will send out 200,000 copies of an enhanced CD with an interactive conflict resolution program, and a Youth Action Guide focused on mentoring and other steps young people can take to prevent youth violence. The guides and CDs will be sent to youth organizations such as after school programs, Boys and Girls Clubs, juvenile justice and law enforcement agencies as part of MTV's yearlong anti-violence campaign. First announced at the White House School Safety Conference last year, the MTV campaign has been educating young people on youth violence issues and linking them to national anti-violence resources."

The President also called on congress to finish the job on guns and hate crimes. The press release continued: "Six months after the tragedy at Columbine High School, the President will call on the Republican leadership now to do its part to reduce youth violence by passing common sense gun legislation. The President will challenge the Congress to finish its work and quickly pass a balanced, bipartisan juvenile crime bill that includes strong gun measures that would: close the gun show loophole; require child safety locks for handguns; ban the importation of large capacity ammunition clips; and bar violent juveniles from owning guns for life.

"The President will also urge Congress to pass the bipartisan Hate Crimes Prevention Act of 1999. This legislation, if enacted, would strengthen current law by making it easier to prosecute crimes based on race, color, religion and national origin and by expanding coverage to include crimes based on sexual orientation, gender and disability."

April 21, 2000

Secretary of Education Richard W. Riley and Attorney General Janet Reno, at the request of President Clinton, reported the response to their 1998 *Early Warning, Timely Response: A Guide to Safe Schools* (the Early Warning Guide).[10] The purpose of this document is to help communities make schools even safer in the future than they are today. Since the release of the guide, the Department of Education received numerous requests for a follow-up resource that provides additional information about the "how to" of developing school safety plans. In response, they developed *Safeguarding Our Children: An Action Guide*. This action guide provides practical steps schools can take to design and implement school safety plans to reduce violence in our schools and help children get access to the services they need. It stresses the importance of a three-stage, comprehensive model that includes prevention, early intervention, and intensive services to address school safety issues. The guide also emphasizes the importance of strategic planning, capacity building, comprehensive approaches, teamwork, and community involvement in successful schools.

This guide was produced by the Center for Effective Collaboration and Practice of the American Institutes for Research, and the National Association for School Psychologists under a cooperative agreement with the United States Department of Education, Office of Special Education and Rehabilitative Services, Office of Special Education Programs. The Office of Elementary and Secondary Education and the Safe and Drug-Free Schools Program provided additional support under the Elementary and Secondary Education Act and the Gun-Free Schools Act. These documents can be downloaded using the Internet site referenced in endnote 10. Relevant portions of these documents will also be synthesized and utilized in Chapters 3 and 4 of this book.

May 2000

On May 12, 2000, Representative Joe Baca introduced legislation in the U.S. House of Representatives that takes a comprehensive approach to preventing school and youth violence.[11] Baca's legislation, the "Comprehensive School Safety Act of 2000," provides grants to state educational agencies to enable schools to develop and implement school safety plans. "The issue of school safety has taken center stage throughout America," Baca said. "School violence can happen anywhere and can be inflicted upon anyone…. Providing safe schools must remain a top priority, and providing comprehensive solutions and programs that focus on prevention need to be enacted," Baca added.

Baca's legislation, H.R. 1216, provides funding for programs to assess the extent of crimes committed on school campuses and at school-related functions; identify appropriate strategies and programs that will provide or maintain a high level of school safety; and, provide each school served the standards to measure and guidelines to ensure a safe and orderly environment that would be conducive to learning. "Our schools must be safe havens for our students and our children," Baca said. "We need to provide safety programs and plans that prevent future violence and tragedies, not simply respond to them." Baca's measure is similar to legislation he authored last year while serving in the California State Senate, SB 195.

"The Comprehensive School Safety Act would incorporate a number of proposals similar to what was contained in SB 195," Baca said. "This includes calling for closed campuses, providing telephone hotlines, intercoms and security video cameras, instituting peer mediation councils and emergency safety drills, and 'character education' curriculum." Baca's legislation will provide parents, students, faculty, school administrators, and any other individuals or groups an opportunity to present their views and make recommendations regarding the development and implementation of a safety plan at each school that receives funding through the program. "I join with all Americans, mothers and fathers, teachers and students, who want an end to the violence in our schools," Baca said. "We need to work together in finding solutions and preventing further violence." On May 8, 2001, the bill was referred to the subcommittee on Education Reform.

March 2001

On March 8, 2001, Congressman Dennis Moore filed a statement supporting legislation on public school safety. The report focused on the following[12]:

"In addition to enforcing existing gun laws, I believe that measures like background checks to keep guns out of the hands of convicted felons should be expanded. I support legislation requiring background checks for gunshow purchases. I am an original sponsor of H.R. 2377, the Gun Show Loophole Closing Act of 2001. This legislation was developed with Senators McCain and Lieberman, who have introduced companion legislation in the Senate (S. 890). This legislation would require gun show background checks at gun shows selling at least 75 guns. Individuals selling guns from their own homes are exempt from this bill. Currently, although 95 percent of all background checks are completed within two hours, the remaining 5 percent take longer because states have not automated all of their conviction records. Recent data indicates that in Kansas only 46 percent of state records for criminal backgrounds are computerized. This legislation would allow up to three days for the maximum allotted time for background checks. Afterwards, states would be allowed to reduce the time for checks to a maximum of 24 hours if they automated up to 95 percent of their criminal records, thus eliminating the need for longer time periods for background checks. This bill has also been referred to the subcommittee on Crime, Terrorism, and Homeland Security.

"Also, trigger locks for guns are a simple way to keep a child from accidentally firing a gun they find in the home. They do not infringe upon Second Amendment rights—and they will save the lives of children. We need to make sure that even if kids do know where the guns are, they can't use them. This isn't about restricting guns; it is about protecting our kids from accidental shootings by requiring the use of trigger locks or other safety devices. The President included in his Fiscal Year 2002 budget request increases of $9 million to hire additional federal gun prosecutors and $75 million to provide safety locks for every handgun in the United States. I support this request, and I will fight for its inclusion in the appropriations process.

"Additionally, in the wake of the Columbine High School tragedy in his district, Representative Tom Tancredo sat down with interested parties in Colorado to form the Colorado School Safety Hotline, a statewide toll-free number manned 24-hours a day that anyone can call to report school violence threats. The Hotline has taken over 972 anonymous calls since its inception in the fall of 1999. Nearly 250 of the calls have been from students, parents, teachers and community members either reporting a threat that was made against the school community or calling to obtain information from the Colorado Bureau of Investigation."

February 2002

On February 11, 2002, Secretary of Education Rod Paige issued a statement to all state school superintendents about school safety.[13] This letter included a document which offers detailed information to bring schools up to date on the specific actions taken by the Department of Education to address the needs of those directly and indirectly affected by the terrorist attacks of September 11, 2001. It also provides several important lessons learned with respect to threat assessment and crisis management in our schools, as well as actions educators and communities can take to implement effective policies to protect our children from both internal and external threats. I encourage you to share this information with members of your staff working on safety and crisis management issues.

The Secretary commented, "Whether we are working to raise expectations for academic achievement or seeking to increase safety within our schools, I am committed to helping you provide an optimistic and hopeful future for every American child."

The document referred to in the Secretary's letter is a PDF file and can be downloaded with Acrobat Reader. See endnote 13 for the Internet reference. Among other things, the enclosure provides information on the following:

- School emergency response to violence
- Trauma response training
- Lessons learned and recommendations from September 11, 2001
- Department of Education activities focusing on school safety issues

February 2002

Also in February 2002, representatives from ten nations gathered in Washington, D.C., to discuss protecting schools from terrorism. During this meeting, the U.S. Department of Education released the following statement[14]: "Following the September 11, 2001, terrorist attacks, public authorities worldwide are learning to adjust to new realities. Government officials from 10 countries—Canada, France, Japan, Israel, Mexico, Ireland, Spain, Turkey, the United Kingdom, and the United States—met in Washington, D.C., on February 13-14, 2002, to discuss strategies for helping schools prepare for and respond to terrorist attacks. Many schools across the United States and around the world have emergency response plans in place that address school violence and natural disasters. This meeting was designed to discuss how government can help schools extend those plans to effectively deal with incidents of terrorism."

Jointly sponsored by the U.S. Department of Education, the U.S. Department of State and the Organization for Economic Co-operation and Development (OECD), the participants used this as an opportunity to:

- Understand the potential for terrorism as a school security issue and to evaluate the risks associated with that issue;
- Learn how other countries are dealing with the issue of possible terrorist attacks on schools and students;
- Identify policies and practices that have worked in the past, as well as those that have not been effective in protecting schools and students from terrorism;

- Identify immediate needs for information exchange, research, technology and training among the participating nations; and
- Establish a network and process for continuing discussion and collaboration.

Judge Eric Andell, senior adviser and counsel to the U.S. Department of Education, chaired the meeting and called it "an exciting and productive opportunity to learn what other countries are doing to address a threat to people of all ages that knows no national boundaries."

The international group of school safety experts also addressed preventive measures, developing regional response plans, training administrators, teachers, students and parents, and helping students to cope with traumatic events. In addition, representatives from New York City and the New York City Board of Education presented an overview of their actions and experiences responding to the terrorist attacks on the World Trade Center. The sponsors of the meeting will release a summary of the discussions as a follow up to this historic international session on school safety.

Sample Recommendations and Laws from State Government

The following provides a sampling of state initiatives and state laws in the area of juvenile violence and school safety. Each of these sections has been edited to provide a capsule view of how each of these states has reacted to school violence in recent years. More information about what these states are doing can be found at the footnoted websites included in the references for this chapter. You are encouraged to explore these pages in more detail. Because of space allocations, only a snapshot is provided here.

Michigan

Model Code of Student Conduct. A Model Code of Student Conduct[15] was developed by the Michigan Department of Education, in collaboration with other state and local agencies, organizations, educators, and concerned citizens, pursuant to Public Act 263 of 2000. This code was founded on the premise that creating safe and drug-free schools requires the commitment of the entire community, including families, schools and community leaders. The Michigan Department of Education encourages each school district to take the lead in bringing all of its community's resources together, to ensure welcoming, safe, gun-free, and drug-free schools.

Adoption of a code of student conduct is one element of a school district's safe schools plan. There is no singular code of student conduct that meets the needs of every school district, although every school district is required by law to adopt a code, as set forth in *The Revised School Code,* MCLA 380.1312(8):

> A local or intermediate school district or a public school academy shall develop and implement a code of student conduct and shall enforce its provisions with regard to pupil misconduct in a classroom, elsewhere on school premises, on a school bus or other school-related vehicle, or at a school sponsored activity or event whether or not it is held on school premises.

This Model Code of Student Conduct is provided as a tool to assist Michigan school districts in developing, updating, or revising their local codes. This document may be modified to reflect local school district policy and procedure.

New York

Firearms Legislation. On August 18, 1998, Governor George E. Pataki increased safety in New York's schools by signing into law legislation allowing 14- and 15-year-old juveniles who possess loaded firearms on school grounds to be prosecuted as adults in criminal court and subjected to tougher penalties.[16] This legislation covers many significant areas of school safety reform. Because of each of these areas is important, providing an extensive coverage of possible criminal activity involving schools and youth, an extensive overview is provided below.

Under the bill, a 14- or 15-year-old who possesses a loaded firearm on school grounds could be sentenced to a maximum term of imprisonment of four years, with a minimum term set at one-third the maximum. A 14- or 15-year-old who possesses a machine gun or loaded firearm with the intent to use the weapon unlawfully against another while on school grounds could be sentenced to a maximum of seven years, with a minimum term set at one-third the maximum.

Under existing law, dangerous weapons include firearms, knives and personal weapons. "School grounds" include the grounds of a public, private, vocational or parochial school, any building, structure, athletic field, playground or land contained within the real property boundary of the school, and also areas accessible to the public within 1000 feet of the school boundary, such as sidewalks, streets, parking lots, parks playgrounds and stores.

Safe Schools Legislation. Also, at the close of the 2000 legislative session, a bill was introduced and passed in New York State known as SAVE, Safe Schools Against Violence in Education legislation.[17] SAVE addresses many important issues that impact on education as well as educators. Included in the SAVE Legislation are:

1. **School Safety Plans:** This will require local schools and law enforcement to develop and adopt district-wide school safety plans and building-level emergency response plans for crisis response and management. Items required include:

> *District-wide school safety teams and building-level emergency response teams;*
>
> *Policies and procedures for responding to threats and acts of violence, safe evacuation and contacting law enforcement and parents during a violent incident, detecting potentially violent persons, building security, and annual school safety training for students and staff.*

2. **Codes of Conduct:** Requires schools to adopt codes of conduct for the maintenance of order on school grounds and to file such codes with the State Education Department (SED). Items include:

> *Appropriate dress and language*
>
> *Security issues*
>
> *Removal from the classroom*
>
> *Discipline procedures*
>
> *Policies and procedures for detention, suspension and teacher removal of disruptive pupils*
>
> *Procedures for reporting and determining code violations and imposing penalties*

This requires a process for reporting violent incidents to law enforcement and requires districts to establish committees to review actions relating to the code.

3. **Disruptive Pupil Removal:** Allows teachers to remove disruptive or violent pupils from the classroom, consistent with district codes of conduct, with appropriate procedural safeguards for affected students.

> *Disruptive pupil* is defined as one who is substantially disruptive of the educational process or interferes with the teacher's authority over the classroom.
>
> *Violent pupil* is defined as one who commits an act of violence on a teacher, other school district employee or fellow student; possesses, displays or threatens to use a gun, knife, or other dangerous weapon; damages or destroys the personal property of a teacher or other school district employee; or damages or destroys school district property.

This bill also adds principals to those empowered to suspend pupils from school entirely, without specific board delegation of that authority. It requires districts to include, in their codes of conduct, minimum periods of suspension for violent or repeatedly disruptive pupils.

4. **Violence Prevention and Intervention Training for Pre-service Professionals:** All persons applying on or after February 2, 2001, for a teaching certificate or license will be required to complete two hours of course work or training in violence prevention and intervention.

5. **Character Education/Health Curriculum/Interpersonal Violence Prevention:** Requires the Board of Regents to include a civility, citizenship and character education component in the K–12 course of instruction concerning the principles of honesty, tolerance, personal responsibility, respect for others, observance of laws and rules, courtesy, dignity and other positive traits.

The Board of Regents must review the current health curriculum requirements to ensure that students have sufficient time and instruction to develop skills to address issues of violence prevention and mental health. The Commissioner of Education must develop and distribute to schools an interpersonal violence prevention package for use in health and related curricula.

6. **Silent Resignations:** Ends the practice of "silent resignations" whereby school authorities allow a person to resign rather than disclosing allegations of child abuse by bringing disciplinary actions through the Education Department or filing a complaint with law enforcement authorities.

If a superintendent permits an employee to resign under these circumstances, it will be a class E felony, punishable by up to a maximum of 4 years in prison. In addition, the superintendent will be subject to a civil penalty not to exceed $20,000.

Individuals who in good faith comply with the reporting requirements will be entitled to immunity from any civil or criminal liability, which might otherwise result from such actions.

7. **Teacher Discipline:** Provides for a range of discipline measures for teachers, consistent with the other professions regulated by the State Education Department. In addition to revocation of a teaching certificate, discipline will now include suspension, continuing education, limitation on certificates and monetary fines.

8. **Prospective Employees and Applicants for Certification:** Requires prospective school district employees and applicants for teacher certification to be fingerprinted for a criminal history background check in order to be cleared for employment at a school or for certification.

9. **Violent Incident Reporting System:** Requires the Commissioner of Education and DCJS to develop a statewide system of reporting violent incidents on school grounds. Schools would report to the Commissioner, at a minimum:

> *The number and types of violent incidents*
> *The number of suspensions and other forms of discipline*
> *Actions taken by the school*
> *Age and grade of disciplined pupils*

This includes an annual report to the Governor and the Legislature regarding the prevalence of violent incidents on school grounds, and inclusion of such information on school report cards.

10. **Court Notification:** Requires family and criminal courts to notify schools about juvenile delinquency adjudications where the student is placed in a youth detention facility, criminal convictions of students and youthful offender adjudications of students. Increases coordination between the juvenile justice system and schools, so that students are better prepared for reintegration into school following release from a youth detention facility.

11. **Whistleblower Protection:** Protection for those employees who report violent incidents, whereby an employee may not be disciplined or fired for reporting these incidents and is protected from any civil liability.

12. **Assaults on Teachers:** Assaults on teachers or school personnel which result in an injury would be increased from a misdemeanor to a Class D felony. The bill increases from a misdemeanor to a Class D felony an assault by a non-student that results in an injury to a student while on school grounds.

13. **Child Abuse in an Educational Setting:** Defines child abuse in an educational setting as any of the following acts committed against a child in an educational setting by a school employee or volunteer:

> *Intentionally or recklessly inflicting physical injury, serious physical injury or death;*
>
> *Intentionally or recklessly engaging in conduct which creates a substantial risk of such physical injury, serious physical injury or death;*
>
> *Any child sexual abuse, defined as any conduct prohibited by Article 130 or 263 of the Penal Law.*

It also requires school employees to report allegations of such abuse to school authorities, parents and law enforcement, in the following manner:

> *Mandatory reporters are teachers, school nurses, guidance counselors, school psychologists, school social workers, school administrators, school board members and any other school personnel required to hold a teaching or administrative license or certificate.*
>
> *Mandatory reporter must prepare a written report of the allegations and transmit it to the school administrator.*
>
> *School administrators who receive such written reports will determine whether there is reasonable cause to believe that child abuse in an educational setting has occurred and, upon making such determination, notify the child's parent and forward the report to appropriate law enforcement authorities.*
>
> *Willful failure to make a required report will be a Class A misdemeanor. Individuals who in good faith comply with the reporting requirements will be entitled to immunity from any civil liability, which might otherwise result from such actions.*

Kentucky

In recent years the state of Kentucky has addressed the problem of school safety and juvenile violence by passing the following laws[18]:

Legislation

Section Number: Ky. Rev. Stat. Ann. § 158.441 (West 1999)

Summary: Defines intervention services as instruction in conflict resolution skills.

Section Number: Ky. Rev. Stat. Ann. § 158.445 (West 1999)

Summary: Requires each local school to begin an assessment of school safety and student discipline during the 1998-99 school year. The assessment should indicate the training needs for staff in classroom management and training needs for students in anger reduction, conflict resolution, peer mediation, and other necessary skills. Each board of education is required to adopt a plan for immediate and long-term strategies to address school safety.

Pending Legislation

Bill Number: 1998 House Bill No. 330
Summary: Establishes the Center for School Safety which will establish a clearinghouse of information concerning school violence prevention; provide training and program development in schools; analyze data; evaluate existing school safety programs; administer grants to local districts; promote interagency efforts to address school discipline and safety issues; prepare and disseminate information regarding best practices in creating safe and effective schools; advise Kentucky Board of Education on administrative policies; and provide annual reports to the governor.
Status: Signed by Governor 4/10/1998

Bill Number: 1999 Kentucky Senate Bill No. 71
Summary: Requires the Kentucky Department of Education to develop and evaluate training materials and guidelines on school safety issues and requires the department to establish and administer a grant program for developing innovative programs for violence prevention and conflict resolution.
Status: Session adjourned, no carryover, 5/18/1998

Bill Number: 2000 Kentucky House Bill No. 803
Summary: Requires each school to begin an assessment of school safety and student discipline codes for clarity and appropriate notice to students and parents including a review of training needs for students in anger reduction, conflict resolution, peer mediation, and other necessary skills.
Status: Session adjourned, no carryover, 5/22/2000

Indiana

Statewide efforts to increase safety in schools received a boost on March 3, 1999, with passage of legislation authored by State Rep. Scott Mellinger (D-Pendleton).[19] By an 85-12 margin, members of the House approved House Bill 1972, which requires each school to designate a specialist to work on safety programs. The bill now moves to the Indiana Senate for additional consideration.

"This bill actually extends efforts initiated by Gov. Frank O'Bannon during the 1997 session of the Indiana General Assembly," Mellinger said. "At that time, he started the Safe Schools program in order to create havens where children could stay. These schools stay open longer hours, usually into the evening, and feature efforts to reduce violent behavior and drug and alcohol abuse, as well as improve academic performance.

"House Bill 1972 expands on this concept by encouraging development of safe school efforts at the local level," he continued. "In addition to requiring a safety specialist at each school corporation, my proposal calls for counties to establish local commissions that would coordinate school safety plans." That coordination would take advantage of resources from law enforcement and the juvenile court system, as well as school administrators. "As much as it disturbs me to say it, the problems caused by drugs and gangs are becoming an ongoing concern throughout our state, not just in our urban areas," Mellinger said.

"Through the Safe School program, we provide a place where kids can go to sharpen their study skills, get advice on careers, and be with friends," he noted. "School safety specialists take these efforts to the next logical step. They would serve as coordinators of all safety and security functions, and develop emergency preparedness plans."

The state would provide the funding for grants to help school corporations develop these safety plans and to hire specialists. "This legislation sets up a system that can help school officials anticipate potential problems, then work on plans that can keep those problems from taking place," Mellinger said. "I am very hopeful this legislation will receive strong support in the Indiana Senate and be signed into law."

Massachusetts

On February 10, 2000, speaking at the first-ever Youth Violence Technical Assistance Forum, Lieutenant Governor Jane Swift reaffirmed the Administration's commitment to school safety across the Commonwealth and announced that $1 million has been designated for cities and towns to combat bullying in their schools.[20]

Swift announced that $1 million will be available for cities and towns across Massachusetts to establish bullying prevention programs. Also part of the Administration's violence prevention plan, the bullying prevention program has been created by the Executive Office of Public Safety to reduce this type of behavior among school children of all ages. By developing clear rules and alerting parents and teachers to problem situations, relationships among students will improve and schools will become safer and more pleasant places for children.

Swift also urged the Legislature to take up the Administration's Violence Free School Zones legislation, which will send a clear message that violence will not be tolerated in schools. The legislation stiffens the penalty for violent crimes committed on school grounds, on a school bus or at a school event. In addition to the sentence already required for a violent crime, this legislation would add an additional one to 10 years behind bars.

Also, $300,000 has been set aside for character education. The Department of Education has begun to include character education in the curriculum of Massachusetts's schools and will create professional development programs to help teachers integrate character into common classes like English and social studies. "Many schools across the Commonwealth have already woven character education into daily lesson plans and have been able to teach children the importance of honesty, discipline, compassion and moderation. Any teacher will tell you that disrespectful, disruptive students are perhaps the biggest barriers to helping the children who are trying to learn," said Swift. "By helping teachers reinforce character and proper behavior, we are not only helping the problem child, but the entire class."

Oregon

On September 25, 1999, reporters Steven Carter and Bill Graves of *The Oregonian* reported that new legislation is now addressing school safety concerns in their state.[21]

Schools have added security guards, ID badges, surveillance cameras and metal detectors. They've cracked down on threats and cast a wary eye on intruders. They also are exploring violence-prevention programs and ways to strengthen the connections between students and staff so alienated kids get helped. Even small rural schools in Oregon practice drills using codes broadcast on intercoms to signal a dangerous intruder in the school.

The Legislature approved one bill that specifically addressed what happened at Thurston High School. It requires that any student taking a gun or weapon on campus be arrested, detained and not released without going before a judge. Had that law been in force in 1998, Kinkel, who pleaded guilty to murder Friday, would not have been released to the custody of his father the day before his shooting spree. State Rep. Bill Morrisette, D-Springfield, who was mayor at the time of the shootings, says the Legislature could have done more to deal with youth violence. But he pointed to Senate Bill 344 as progress. "It

takes the pressure off the arresting officer as to whether there is a prob-
able cause to hold a student," said Morrisette, a former teacher in
Springfield. "In the case of Kip Kinkel, they said, 'He comes from a
great family,' so they let him go."

Lawmakers also approved laws aimed at improving communication between juvenile authorities and schools about potentially violent youths. Police must notify schools when a youth is arrested or a
teen-ager on probation transfers to a new school district. In turn,
schools now must report to police if any staffer suspects a student has
been on campus with a gun or other destructive device. And they must
set clear policies on how to deal with children who threaten or actually harm their peers. That could include immediate removal from
class and psychological evaluation. That law also included a provision
requiring schools to notify parents if their children's names turn up
on a "hit list" of any angry student.

Also approved was a package aimed at preventing violence among
at-risk children. The bill requires juvenile authorities, law enforcement agencies and schools to do joint planning at the county level to
reduce youth violence, which some of them are already doing.

North Carolina

In North Carolina, school safety legislation covers students, juvenile law, and preventive measures[22]:

Student Discipline. Everyone agrees that schools should be safe and
orderly. In response, the General Assembly in recent years has made several significant changes to the statutes governing student suspension and
expulsion. S.L. 1998-220 makes several additional changes to the suspension statutes.
  • An amendment to G.S. 115C-391(d) permits the local school super-
    intendent as well as the local board of education to suspend a stu-
    dent who brings a weapon onto school property for 365 days.
  • G.S. 115C-391(d2) now makes the superintendent, not the local
    board of education, responsible for suspending or removing to an
    alternative educational setting a student who commits an assault
    under circumstances covered by this statute.
  • G.S. 115C-391(e) now provides that a superintendent's decision under
    G.S. 115C-391(c) (suspension longer than ten days), 115C-391(d1)
    (suspension for bringing a weapon), or 115C-391(d2) (suspension or
    removal to an alternative educational setting for certain assaults) may

be appealed to the local board of education. Expulsion [G.S. 115C-391(d)] remains a decision of the local board of education.

- Superintendents had been required to keep data on *all* students who were expelled or suspended. G.S. 115C-276(r) now provides that superintendents must keep data on students who are expelled or suspended *for more than ten days.*

Rewrite of the Juvenile Code. The Juvenile Justice Reform Act, S.L. 1998-202 (S 1260), is a complete rewrite of the Juvenile Code, which is now codified as G.S. Chapter 7B and which becomes effective July 1, 1999. Chapter 13 (Juvenile Law) explains all of these changes in detail. Several provisions that affect schools directly are discussed below. One should go to the website listed in footnote 22 and click on Chapter 13 to read the entire text of this law.

Information Sharing among Agencies. New G.S. 7B-3100 permits the Office of Juvenile Justice, after consultation with the Conference of Chief District Court Judges, to adopt rules designating certain local agencies that are authorized to share information about juveniles. Upon request, these agencies must share with one another information they possess that is relevant to any case in which a petition is filed alleging that a juvenile is abused, neglected, dependent, undisciplined, or delinquent. This sharing of information must continue until the juvenile is no longer subject to the jurisdiction of juvenile court. Local school administrative units are among the agencies authorized to share information. Agencies may use this shared information only for the protection of the juvenile or others or to improve the educational opportunities of the juvenile and may release the information only in accordance with the federal Family Educational Rights and Privacy Act.

Notification to Schools of Juvenile Crimes. New G.S. 7B-3101, which requires notification of school principals in certain circumstances involving juveniles, does not change the law specifying when schools will receive notice. It simply recodifies former law (G.S. 7A-675.2) and directs principals to handle any notification in accordance with G.S. 115C-404, as amended by S.L. 1998-202. The principal must destroy documents received in accordance with G.S. 7B-3101 when the principal receives notification that the court has dismissed the petition, transferred jurisdiction over the student to superior court, or granted the student's petition for expunction of the records. The principal must destroy all information gained from examination of juvenile records in accordance with G.S. 7B-3101 when the principal finds that the school no longer needs the information to protect the safety of or improve educational opportunities for the student or others. If the student graduates, withdraws from school, is suspended for the remainder of the school year, is expelled, or transfers to another school, the principal must return all remaining documents to the juvenile court counselor. Information gained by the school in accordance with G.S. 7B-3101 may not be the sole basis for a decision to suspend or expel a student.

Program on Prevention of Abuse and Neglect. G.S. 7B-1301 requires the State Board of Education, through the Department of Public Instruction, to implement the Program on Prevention of Abuse and Neglect. The board must contract with public or private nonprofit organizations, agencies, schools, or individuals to operate community-based educational and service programs designed to prevent abuse and neglect. The programs and services should impact juveniles and families before any substantiated incident of abuse or neglect has occurred. These programs may include community-based educational programs on prenatal care, parental bonding, child development, basic child care, care of children with special needs, and coping with family stress; community-based programs relating to crisis care; and support groups for families experiencing stress. Funding for the prevention programs will come from the Children's Trust Fund in the Department of State Treasurer. In addition, the State Board of Education must develop a state plan for the prevention of abuse and neglect for submission to the Governor, President of the Senate, and Speaker of the House of Representatives.

California

In California a comprehensive package of legislation was written in response to school safety needs[23]:

School Safety
SB 16 (Knight-R) **Crime: Terrorizing**—Amends the statute proscribing arson or bombing in particular situations with intent to terrorize to include arson or bombing of schools.

    Chapter 212, Statutes of 1997
    SB 187 (Hughes-D) **Comprehensive School Safety Plans**—Requires school districts and county offices of education to develop comprehensive school safety plans, as specified.

    Chapter 736, Statutes of 1997
    SB 366* (Hughes-D) **Commission on Peace Officer Standards and Training**—Requires the Commission on Peace Officer Standards and Training to review minimum training and selection standards for school peace officers. Authorizes reimbursement for the specified training of nonsworn personnel.

    Chapter 117, Statutes of 1997
    SCR 10 (Hughes-D) **School Conduct and Safety**—Recognizes that all public school pupils and employees have certain specified rights regarding high standards for conduct, safety and academic achievement.

    Resolution Chapter 48, Statutes of 1997
    SCR 49 (Hughes-D) **School Safety Month and Yellow Ribbon Week**—Proclaims October 1997 as School Safety Month and January 12 through

January 16, 1998, as Yellow Ribbon Week to demonstrate a commitment to school safety.

Resolution Chapter 118, Statutes of 1997
AB 307 (Kaloogian-R) **Pupils: Suspension and Expulsion**—Adds terrorist threats against school officials or school property to the list of actions for which a principal or superintendent may suspend a pupil or recommend him or her for expulsion.

Chapter 405, Statutes of 1997
AB 367 (Havice-D) **Community Policing and Mentoring for School Safety**—Creates the Community Policing and Mentoring for School Safety Pilot Program to provide 2-year grants to 2 specified school districts in support of school and law enforcement agency partnerships.

Chapter 935, Statutes of 1997
AB 412 (Wildman-D) **Pupils: Suspension and Expulsion**—Requires school districts to report the specific offenses for which pupils are suspended or expelled, and makes a clarification to the list of acts for which a pupil may be suspended or expelled.

Chapter 637, Statutes of 1997
AB 431 (Baldwin-R) **Pupil Expulsion**—Modifies the requirement for the expulsion of a student enrolled in K through 6, inclusive, upon a finding that the pupil committed an act specified in the "zero-tolerance" law enacted in 1995.

(On Senate Inactive File)
AB 676 (Strom-Martin-D) **School Safety**—Requires that any new or modernized school funded from the state school facilities program after January 1, 1998, include a telephone connection in each classroom.

Vetoed by the Governor
AB 1003 (Thompson-R) **School Districts**—Requires every school district governing board to adopt a policy to notify, as soon as possible, pupils and parents of a school when a felony is committed on or near the school campus and the victim of the crime is either a student attending a school or is an employee of the district.

(In Assembly Appropriations Committee)
AB 1253 (Perata-D) **Comprehensive School Site Safety Plan Program**—Establishes the Comprehensive School site Safety Plan Program as a 2-year pilot program to create a model program for the development and establishment of comprehensive school site safety plans in school districts. Appropriates $10 million from the General Fund for the 1997-98 fiscal year for allocation to school districts.

(In Assembly Education Committee)
AB 1351 (Morrow R) **Pupil Expulsion**—Allows school districts to sus-

pend or expel pupils who commit specified offenses in times and places unrelated to school activities.

Texas

Legislative initiatives in Texas have included the following.[24]
SCR 79 by Ratliff
Code Section Impacted: None.
Summary: The Resolution directs the Texas Department of Health, in collaboration with the Texas Education Agency, the Texas Department of Human Services, the Texas Department of Mental Health and Mental Retardation, the Texas Commission on Alcohol and Drug Abuse, the Texas Department of Public Safety, the Department of Protective and Regulatory Services, the Criminal Justice Policy Council, and the office of the Attorney General, within existing resources, to lead an inquiry into youth violence in this state, both real and potential, including the incidence and root causes of such violence and ways by which such violence can be prevented. This inquiry should include, at a minimum, participation of parents, children, actual classroom teachers, and school counselors. The agencies must submit a full report of their findings and recommendations to the 77th Legislature when it convenes in January 2001.

Future implications: The recommendations to the 77th Legislature may lead to law changes that will reduce violence in schools and communities in Texas.

Outstanding issues: None
Does this bill create a new program? No.
Does this bill require a new report? The agencies must submit a full report of their finding and recommendations to the 77th Legislature when it convenes in January 2001.
Does this bill require that rules be adopted? No.

Indiana

On January 19, 2000, an Indiana House Committee approved legislation authored by State Rep. Claire Leuck (D-Fowler) that will benefit school security throughout the state.[25] The Committee on Education approved House Bill 1074 by a unanimous vote. The proposed legislation calls for an executive session to be held to discuss the assessment, design and implementation of school security and safety matters. "The importance of school security has become apparent in this day and age," said Leuck. The second part of the legislation would make school safety and security measures, plans and systems confidential. Public agencies would have the discretion of keeping the confidentiality of the security plans. The proposed legislation has no fiscal impact and will be considered next by the full House.

Fourth Amendment Issues and Students' Rights

In May 1997, Dorianne Beyer, general counsel, National Child Labor Committee, filed a report concerning "School Safety and the Legal Rights of Students." A digest of the report from ERIC (Educational Resources Information Center) presents a brief review of recent Fourth Amendment decisions that affect the rights of students regarding searches and seizures and the parameters of schools' authority to maintain a crime-free environment.[26] This report provides substantial background on Fourth Amendment issues and student rights and concerned with the following issues:

- Cases involving the delicate balance between students' rights and school safety procedures,
- Protections against unreasonable searches and seizures,
- The interpretation of "reasonable suspicion," and
- Searches that are performed with malicious intent to deprive students of their rights.

The report stated:

Some recent search cases in which the two-pronged "reasonableness test" was successfully applied include these:
- A school dance monitor, who, upon seeing that some students were inebriated, in contravention of school policy, took them to a private office and asked them to blow on her face (*Martinez v. School District No. 60*, 1992).
- Upon hearing an unusual thud when a student threw his bag onto a metal cabinet, a security guard rubbed his hand along the bag to feel for a gun (Matter of Gregory M., 1992/1993).

- Upon a student's report to a guidance counselor that another student possessed an illicit drug, the administrator searched the latter student's book bag, because the administrator also had knowledge that the student had been previously disciplined for possession of a controlled substance (*State v. Moore*, 1992).

The case law on student search and seizure has yielded a few other useful factors to consider when conducting a search to ensure that it is reasonable at the inception and in scope. They include the student's age, history, and school record; the seriousness and pervasiveness as a school problem of the suspected infraction or crime; the urgency that required the search without delay; the school official's prior experience with the student; and the evidentiary value and reliability of the information used to justify the search (Rapp, 1994).

What cannot and will not be condoned by the courts are searches that are performed with malicious intent to deprive students of their rights, those where school officials know or should have known that their actions violated students' rights, those that are capricious or discriminatory, and those that do not closely follow school search policies.

The T.L.O. rule (that students are citizens covered by the Fourth Amendment [*New Jersey v. T.L.O.*, 1985] and school officials, when acting in furtherance of publicly mandated educational and disciplinary policies, far more akin to government agents—the very subject of Fourth Amendment restrictions—than to parental surrogates who, under the doctrine of *in loco parentis*, were free from constitutional restraints) and its progeny have been applied to the rights of school authorities to engage in the following acts:

- Search students' school lockers to look for contraband or illegal materials (Student searches and the law, 1995; *S.C. v. State*, 1991).
- Search a student's car in the school parking lot (*State v. Slattery*, 1990; Student searches and the law, 1995).
- Organize searches by drug-sniffing dogs (*Doe v. Renfrow*, 1980; *Horton v. Goose Creek Independent School District*, 1982; *Jennings v. Joshua Independent School District*, 1989; *Jones v. Latexo Independent School District*, 1980) or metal detector machines (*People v. Dukes*, 1992; *National Treasury Employers Union v. Van Raab*, 1989).
- Perform a visual or manual body cavity search (Student searches and the law, 1995).

With reference to drug testing, the report included the following observations:

As contentious as Fourth Amendment issues have been, the lessons of the

T.L.O. case were not substantially reviewed until the courts assessed the issue of mandatory and voluntary drug testing. Until 1995, the short answer to the question of whether schools could mandate all or a class of students to submit to blood or urine tests for drugs could be clearly answered: "no" (Price, 1988). Such testing was seen as a violation of students' reasonable expectation of privacy (*Jones v. McKenzie*, 1986), and repugnant not only to the U.S. Constitution, but also to the nation's common sense of students' integrity (*Anable v. Ford*, 1985; *Odenheim v. Carlstadt–East Ruther-ford Regional School District*, 1985). The courts did, however, make a distinction between mandatory and voluntary drug testing, with the latter subject to no Fourth Amendment protections, as it is based upon consent.

That distinction blurs, though, when the tests are used as a precondition for school enrollment or for participation in extracurricular activities. Until June 27, 1995, the courts were split on drug testing as a precondition for participating in extracurricular activities, with some courts approving it exactly because these activities are voluntary (Student Searches and the Law, 1995). Then came *Acton v. Vernonia School District 47J* (1991), which involved a high school student, James Acton, who wanted to be on his school's football team. His parents refused to sign a form consenting to a urinalysis that would test their son for a variety of drugs, if James were randomly selected by school authorities to comply with the school's newly instituted mandatory, random drug testing program. There was no claim that James was suspected of drug use, but school authorities asserted that their random urinalysis drug testing policy was the result of their being at their "wits' end" over how to solve a perceived growing drug problem (Daniels, 1995).

James Acton, as a consequence of his parents' refusal to consent to such a test, was denied a spot on the football team. In courtroom after courtroom, ending at the U.S. Supreme Court, school officials pressed their claim that they were justified in implementing their random testing program in order to stop the rowdy, anti-authoritarian behavior of their athletic teams that resulted from increased drug use in their rural Oregon school. The 9th Circuit Court of Appeals agreed with the Actons, found the mandatory policy an 'unreasonable search,' and rousingly stated that "children, students, do not have to surrender their right to privacy in order to secure their right to participate in athletics."

Endnote 26 provides the Internet site where this complete report can be found. The school administrator interested in school law as related to students' rights, especially where school safety is a concern, should download this quite lengthy report and follow the case laws in their entirety.

Federal Support for
Improving School Safety

Kevin Mitchell, co-editor of *The ERIC Review* and a writer and editor for ACCESS ERIC in Rockville, Maryland, filed the following report about federal support for improving school safety[27]:

Ensuring the safety of all students requires the collaborative efforts of the entire community. This section of "The ERIC Review" describes federal support for school safety and violence prevention programs, presents a sample of model programs that educators can implement in their classrooms, and provides information resources for educators, parents, researchers, and others interested in learning more about these topics. We hope that you will find these resources helpful as a starting point for further investigation.

The federal government continues to show strong support for programs and initiatives designed to improve the safety of U.S. schools. One of the seven priorities of the U.S. Department of Education (ED) is to ensure that every school in the United States will be strong, safe, drug free, and disciplined. Other agencies, particularly the U.S. Department of Justice (DOJ), have also devoted extensive resources to this goal. The following discussion provides an overview of these federal efforts.

Safe and Drug-Free Schools Program

ED sponsors the Safe and Drug-Free Schools Program (http://www.ed. gov/offices/OESE/SDFS), the federal government's primary vehicle for meeting the seventh priority through education and prevention activities in the schools. The Safe and Drug-Free Schools Program administers initiatives and activities authorized by Title IV of the Improving America's Schools Act of 1994. The Safe and Drug-Free Schools Program consists of two major components: National Programs and State Grants for Drug and Violence Prevention Programs.

Safe and Drug-Free Schools National Programs support a variety of discretionary activities that respond to emerging needs. Many of these activities are prevention projects coordinated by several federal agencies. For example, ED, DOJ, the U.S. Department of Health and Human Services (HHS), the National Institute of Mental Health, the Office of Management and Budget, and the Federal Emergency Management Agency all support Project SERV (School Emergency Response to Violence). Project SERV, proposed by President Clinton in 1998, would help school districts and communities cope with the consequences of major acts of violence by providing training and technical assistance, identifying best practices, and improving coordination at the federal, state, and local levels.

Grants

ED supports a number of grants through the Safe and Drug-Free Schools National Programs. For example, ED awards competitive grants to approximately 120 school districts for activities that promote safe and drug-free learning environments. Grantees are required to demonstrate that their schools have severe drug or safety problems and to implement related research-based programs and strategies that address those problems. In addition, ED funds continuation awards for grants to improve the effectiveness of prevention programming for youth.

Through the Safe and Drug-Free Schools State Grants for Drug and Violence Prevention Programs, ED supports drug and violence prevention in almost every school district and community in the United States. For more information on these and other drug and violence prevention grants offered through the Safe and Drug-Free Schools Program, see the Web site at http://www.ed.gov/offices/OESE/SDFS/grants.html. For general information on ED's grant opportunities, see *What Should I Know About ED Grants?* (http://www.ed.gov/pubs/KnowAbtGrants) and *Guide to U.S. Department of Education Programs and Resources* (http://web99.ed. gov/GTEP/Program2.nsf).

Initiatives

ED also supports several initiatives to promote safe schools. For example, the Middle School Coordinator Initiative allows school districts to hire and train school safety coordinators who will improve drug and violence prevention programs in middle schools. The Safe Schools/Healthy Students Initiative, a joint project of ED, DOJ, and HHS, helps schools and communities implement and enhance community-wide strategies for creating safe and drug-free schools and for promoting healthy childhood development. ED also supports the National School Safety Training Program for Teachers and Educational Personnel [created] in June 1999. ED, DOJ, and HHS will participate in this program by developing training sessions, distributing materials, coordinating outreach programs, and providing technical assistance to the National Education Association and other partners.

For more information on school safety initiatives, see the Safe and Drug-Free Schools Program's Web site at http://www.ed.gov/offices/OESE/SDFS. To stay abreast of all education initiatives, see ED's Web site at http://www.ed.gov/pubs/EDInitiatives.

Information, Training, and Technical Assistance

ED and several other federal agencies support safe, drug-free schools by providing information, training, and technical assistance to schools and their surrounding communities. For example, ED and DOJ support the

National Resource Center for Safe Schools (http://www.safetyzone.org), which provides online access to related databases, publications, funding opportunities, and Web sites, in addition to training and technical assistance.

The National Center for Conflict Resolution Education (http://www.nccre.org), another joint project of ED and DOJ, provides training and technical assistance to advance the development of conflict resolution education programs in a variety of settings, including schools, juvenile justice settings, and youth service organizations.

In addition, ED funds the Educational Resources Information Center (ERIC) through the Office of Educational Research and Improvement and the National Library of Education. ERIC maintains the world's largest education database, which includes a wealth of information on school safety and on drug and violence prevention. Several of the ERIC Clearinghouses, including Counseling and Student Services (http://www.uncg.edu/edu/ericcass), Educational Management (http://eric.uoregon.edu), and Urban Education (http://eric-web.tc.columbia.edu), provide relevant online resources and information. In addition, the AskERIC Web site (http://www.askeric.org) provides many resources related to school safety, including links to relevant Web sites, e-mail lists, and ERIC publications.

Other federal and federally funded organizations that provide information and other resources related to school safety include the Center for Mental Health in Schools (http://smhp.psych.ucla.edu), the Center for Effective Collaboration and Practice (http://www.air-dc.org/cecp), and DOJ's Office of Juvenile Justice and Delinquency Prevention (http://ojjdp.ncjrs.org/resources/topic.html).

Publications

ED publishes many excellent publications on school safety and on drug and violence prevention, including the *Annual Report on School Safety; Indicators of School Crime and Safety, 1998; Early Warning, Timely Response: A Guide to Safe Schools; Creating Safe and Drug-Free Schools: An Action Guide; and Protecting Students from Harassment and Hate Crime: A Guide for Schools.* Readers can link to online versions of these publications from ED's Web site at: http://www.ed.gov/offices/OESE/SDFS/safeschools.html.

In addition, all of ED's current free publications and products are available through ED's Publications Center (ED Pubs). Visitors to the ED Pubs Web site (http://www.ed.gov/pubs/edpubs.html) can search the online catalog by title or browse by subject. All items can also be ordered by calling toll free 1-877-433-7827. For more information on ED's various activities, initiatives, publications, and partnerships related to school safety, see ED's Web site at http://www.ed.gov/offices/OESE/SDFS/edresp.html.

3

Strategies for Building a School Safety Program

After surveying the responses and recommendations from federal and state authorities, we can now turn our attention to constructing the parameters of a school safety program. Notwithstanding the hierarchy of public school districts, and understanding that most school safety programs will be generated from federal, state, and district funding down to the school level, the recommended strategies in this chapter will concentrate on the school. It is at the school level where we find students and teachers engaged in the struggle to learn, develop socially, and finally emerge as civil adults. Here is where the fulcrum of student activity occurs, both violent and nonviolent. Here is where we apply our best strategies for school safety.

In order to apply effective prevention strategies and programs, we must first differentiate between effective and ineffective ones, apply scientific standards for what works, and then narrow these approaches to model programs (see Chapter 4). According to the Surgeon General's report on youth violence, "The strategy of using prevention resources to their fullest potential presents many challenges. The first lies in identifying effective prevention approaches and programs. Differentiating between effective and ineffective ones can be a difficult chore for schools, communities, and juvenile justice authorities."[1] The Surgeon General's report noted that many groups and agencies have published recommendations on "what works" in youth violence prevention, "but in many cases there is little consistency regarding the specific programs they recommend."

The approach chosen by the Surgeon General's report is less empirical than a rigorous statistical, meta-analysis one. It is based on a review of the evaluation research of effective programs and identifies the general strategies that characterize them. While this approach is not quantitative, the research is easily conducted and offers useful information for generating hypotheses and drawing conclusions about the effectiveness of the strategies used for preventing youth violence. This method identifies "best practices," and relies heavily on published reviews which focus on strategies and programs which have demonstrated positive effects on preventing youth violence. (See the Appendix for a list of resources used in this report.) The Surgeon General points out that acknowledging that certain programs and strategies have demonstrated effectiveness does not mean that other approaches are unimportant. The report hypothesizes, "Programs that successfully address multiple risk factors, even those with very small individual effect sizes, may be very useful and should be supported and disseminated. Given limited funding, however, it seems prudent to invest in those programs that have greater potential effects on violence prevention."

The scientific standards for judging violence prevention programs include (1) rigorous experimental design, (2) evidence of significant deterrent effects, and (3) replication (the requirement of sustainability) of these effects at multiple sites or in clinical trials. The report says, "High-quality evaluations of youth violence prevention programs should be designed to demonstrate with this degree of confidence that a program is reducing the onset or prevalence of violent behavior or individual rates of offending. Since serious delinquency is strongly related to violence, reductions in serious criminal behavior (or index crimes) are also considered to be acceptable outcome measures for identifying effective violence prevention programs."[2] The report concludes, "Before a program is recommended and funded for national implementation, it is important to show clearly that it has a significant, sustained preventive or deterrent effect and that it can be expected to have positive results in a wide range of community settings."[3]

Strategies and Programs — Requirements

One should understand the difference between "prevention" and "intervention." True or *primary prevention* is defined as "lessening the likelihood that youths in a treatment or intervention program will initiate violent behavior, compared to a control group." Prevention programs are therefore designed to target youths who have not yet become involved in violence or encountered specific risk factors for violence. On the other hand, intervention is defined as "reducing the risk of violence among youths who display one or more risk factors for violence (high-risk students) or preventing further violence or the escalation of violence among youths who are already involved in violent behavior." These interventions are known as *secondary* and *tertiary prevention*. The targeted youths are those identified as high-risk or those already violent. There will be some overlap between prevention and intervention programs. The difference is that programs that have been effective in general populations for preventing violent behavior are not always effective in reducing further violence among seriously delinquent youths.

Primary Prevention Programs

Primary youth violence prevention programs aim to prevent the onset of youth violence and related risk factors. These programs may change individual risk factors, target environmental factors, or both. The Surgeon General's research report found that skills-oriented programs are among the most effective strategies for reducing youth violence and risk factors for youth violence. The model program, which matches this approach and is mentioned in the report, is Life Skills Training and the Midwestern Prevention Project (see Chapter 4).

SOCIAL SKILLS

Life Skills Training (LST) is designed to prevent or reduce drug use among middle or junior high age students from grades six through nine. The primary focus is in grades six and seven with additional sessions in grades eight and nine. There are three major components to the curriculum: self-management skills, social skills, and information and skills related specifically to drug use. Teaching techniques include direct instruction, demonstrations, feedback, reinforcement, and practice. Evaluations show that students who participate in Life Skills Training have a lower risk of drug use, smoking, and inhalant, narcotic, and hallucinogen use.

Several programs are mentioned which fit this model. **The Midwestern Prevention Project** targets students in grades six and seven with the goal of preventing or reducing the risk of gateway drug use associated with the transition from early adolescence to middle through late adolescence. The program trains students to avoid drug use and the situations where drugs are most likely to be used. The program includes five components: mass media program, school program, parent education and organization, community organization, and local health policy. This program has demonstrated positive effects in reducing daily smoking and marijuana use, hard drug use, and smoking through age twenty-three. Also, evaluations have shown that this program has facilitated improvements in parent-child communication about drug use and in the development of prevention programs, activities, and services within communities.

Additional life skills training programs include two school-based programs that focus on teaching social skills. Each of these meet the criteria for a promising program. The **Promoting Alternative Thinking Strategies (PATHS)** curriculum is taught to elementary school students beginning at grade five. Lessons focus on emotional competence, self-control, social competence, positive peer relations, and interpersonal problem-solving skills. These lessons are taught three times a week in 20- to 30-minute sessions. Evaluations have shown that PATHS has positive effects on several risk factors associated with violence. These include aggressive behavior, anxiety and depression, conduct problems, and lack of self-control. Both regular students and special students have benefited from this program.

I Can Problem Solve has been used effectively with students in nursery school, kindergarten, and in grades five and six. Twelve group sessions taught over three months trains students to use problem-solving skills to find solutions to interpersonal problems. Evaluations have shown a positive effect on improving classroom behavior and problem-solving skills for up to four years after the end of the intervention. Also, evaluations show that the program is effective with all children, but is most effective with children living in poor, urban areas.

INVOLVING PARENTS

Training programs for parents have also been shown to strengthen skills-training programs when taught in tandem. Two programs have shown promise: the **Iowa Strengthening Families Program** and **Preparing for the Drug-Free Years**. These are family-based rather than school-based programs.

The **Iowa Strengthening Families Program** targets sixth graders and their families in seven weekly sessions designed to improve parenting skills and family communication. The program has been evaluated in rural, midwestern schools with primarily white, middle-class students. **Preparing for the Drug-Free Years** is a family competency-training program that promotes healthy, protective parent-child interactions and includes skills training for youths. This program includes one session focusing on peer pressure (students and parents included), and four parent-only sessions: risk factors and family protective factors for adolescent substance use, effective parenting skills, managing anger and family conflict, and facilitating positive child involvement in family activities. These programs have demonstrated positive effects on child-family relationships and avoidance of alcohol, tobacco, and marijuana use for up to four years after participation.

Another promising family-oriented program is **Linking the Interests of Families and Teachers (LIFT)**. This program combines school-based skills training for children with parent training. The classroom component of the program aims at first grade through fifth grade students and involves twenty one-hour sessions delivered over ten weeks. There is a peer component focusing on positive social behavior during playground activities. The parent component involves parent sessions on reducing children's antisocial behaviors, involvement with delinquent peers, and drug and alcohol use. Evaluations have shown that students who participate in LIFT exhibit less physical aggression on the playground, exhibit better social skills, and are less likely to associate with delinquent peers, use alcohol, or be arrested.

SHAPING BEHAVIOR

Behavior management programs have also confirmed consistent effects on violence, delinquency, and related risk factors. These programs are usually school-based and include behavior monitoring and the reinforcement of attendance, academic progress and school behavior, and behavioral techniques for classroom management. Research studies provide evidence that interventions focusing on enhancing pos itive student behavior, attendance, and academic achievement through consistent rewards and monitoring can reduce substance use, self-reported criminal activity, and arrests, as well as enhance academic achievements in middle school students.[4] For example, in one study students exposed to behavior management intervention programs were far less likely than students in a control group to have a delinquency record five years after the program ended.

Behavioral techniques for classroom management represent a general strategy for changing the classroom environment. The best strategies for promoting positive classroom behavior are establishing clear rules and directions, use of praise and approval, behavior modeling, token reinforcement, self-specification of contingencies, self-reinforcement, and behavior shaping.[5] This program includes strategies aimed at reducing negative student behaviors, including: ignoring misbehavior, reinforcing behavior that is incompatible with negative behavior, relaxation methods, and using disciplinary techniques such as soft reprimands, timeouts, and point losses and fines in token economies.

The Seattle Social Development Project (SSDP) is the example the Surgeon General's report highlights that includes classroom behavior management among its core components. The goal of SSDP is to enhance elementary school students' bonds with their school and their families while decreasing a number of risk factors for violence. The Surgeon General's report includes SSDP among its model programs because it includes both individual and environmental change approaches and multiple components known to improve the effectiveness of violence prevention. There are three components to the program: classroom behavior management, child skills training, and parent training. Evaluations have shown that SSDP reduces the initiation of alcohol, marijuana, and tobacco use by grade six and improves attachment and commitment to school. Because the program targets prosocial behavior, interpersonal problem-solving, academic success, and avoidance of drug use, at age eighteen, youths who participated in the full five-year version of this program have, at age eighteen, lower rates of violence, heavy drinking, and sexual activity, and better academic performance than controls. SSDP has been used successfully in both general populations of youths and high-risk children attending elementary and middle school.

Focusing on classroom behavior, the Surgeon General's report points to three promising programs: the Bullying Prevention Program, the Good Behavior Game, and the School Transitional Environmental Program. The **Bullying Prevention Program** targets elementary and middle school (junior high) students beginning with an anonymous student questionnaire designed to assess bullying problems in individual schools. Using the information from this questionnaire, parents and teachers implement school-, classroom-, and individual-level interventions designed to address the bullying problems that have been identified. At the classroom level, teachers and students work together to establish and reinforce a set of rules about behavior and bullying, creating a positive, anti-bullying climate. This program is designed to change both individual behaviors and environmental factors that prevent nonviolence in the school and on the playground. Evidence has shown that bullying and other anti-social behavior, including theft, vandalism, and truancy, dropped as a result of this program. Begun in Norway, replications have been conducted in England, Germany, and the United States with similar results.

The **Good Behavior Game**, like the Bullying Prevention Program, uses classroom behavior management as the primary means of reducing problem behaviors. This game focuses on elementary school students and is designed to improve their psychological well-being and decrease early aggressive and antisocial behavior. Research has confirmed that these programs are able to reduce antisocial behavior, but their effects on violence and delinquency have not yet been calculated. Teachers have reported positive effects using these programs to reduce aggressive and shy behaviors in first-graders. Long-term evaluations show sustained decreases in aggression among boys rated most aggressive in the first grade, but the effects of this program on violence and delinquency have not been measured.

Another promising primary intervention program also uses classroom behavior management. It is the **School Transitional Environmental Program (STEP)**. STEP is based on the Transitional Life Events Model, which hypothesizes that those stressful life events—such as transitions between schools—places children at risk of troubled behavior. The goal of this program is to reduce the stress and disorganization often associated with changing schools by redefining the role of homeroom teachers. The program uses behavior management "to create an environment that promotes academic achievement and reduces school behavior problems and absenteeism." Research shows that when students fully participate in this program, both substance abuse and delinquency are reduced while academic achievement and school dropout rates are improved. The STEP program has been shown to be effective with entering junior and senior high school students in urban, predominantly nonwhite communities. Effectiveness has also been demonstrated with students who have behavioral problems and are considered to be "high risk."

EMPOWERING SCHOOLS

Capacity-building programs at the school level have been effective in reducing youth violence and related outcomes. Capacity-building programs are those that concentrate on the school's capacity to plan, implement, and sustain positive changes. When these programs are sustained over time, they can significantly reduce student delinquency and drug use. When students, parents, community leaders, and school personnel cooperate to organize, plan, initiate, and sustain school change to reduce violence and drug use, positive effects have been demonstrated, especially on delinquency rates. Such programs empower students to address school safety problems with demonstrated reductions in fighting and teacher victimization.

TEACHING STRATEGIES

Teaching strategies such as continuous progress programs and cooperative learning are also effective at reducing the risk of academic failure—a risk factor for youth violence. Continuous progress programs focus on skill development, allowing students to proceed through a hierarchy of skills and advancing to the next level as each skill is learned. This approach eliminates the problem of school failure and has shown to have positive effects on academic achievement in elementary school in seven separate evaluations.

Cooperative learning has been in schools since the mid–1980s. It is a teaching strategy that includes a variety of techniques designed to improve academic achievement in elementary school children. Cooperative learning programs place students of various skill levels together in small groups, allowing students to help each other learn. Evaluations have shown that this approach to teaching and learning has had positive effects on attitudes toward school, race relations, attitudes toward mainstreamed exceptional education students, and on academic achievement.[6]

COMMUNITY INITIATIVES

Community-based programs, such as positive youth development programs, have also had positive effects on youth violence. While evaluations are ongoing for these types of programs (Boys and Girls Clubs and Big Brothers and Big Sisters of America programs), the evidence is strong enough to conclude that they are effective at reducing youth violence and violence-related outcomes. Evaluations of Boys and Girls Clubs have shown reductions in vandalism, drug trafficking, and youth crime. An evaluation of a Canadian after-school program has shown large reductions in arrests. Community-based programs may be considered primary prevention programs and also secondary prevention programs, since the specific youth development programs listed above are usually implemented in high-risk neighborhoods.

Ineffective Primary Prevention Programs

Current research has shown that there are some educational approaches that target universal populations that have a consistent lack of effect in scientific studies. The Surgeon General's report mentions the following school-based programs that have no demonstrated effectiveness on youth violence. First among these are peer-led programs such as peer counseling, peer mediation, and peer leaders. The report says, "In a 1987 review of these interventions, Gottfredson concluded that there is no evidence of a positive effect and that these strategies can actually harm high school students."[7] These results were confirmed by a meta-analysis. The analysis concluded that adult-led programs are as effective as, or more effective than, peer-led programs in reducing youth violence. Another measure that has shown to be ineffective and may have harmful effects is nonpromotion to succeeding grades. Generally, nonpromotion to succeeding grades has a negative effect on student achievement, attendance, behavior, and attitudes toward school.

The Surgeon General's research team concluded that the program **Drug Abuse Resistance Education (DARE)** meets the criteria for *Does Not Work*. DARE is the most widely used youth drug prevention program in the United States. Parents, teachers, police, and government funding agencies substantially support it. Numerous studies, meta-analyses, and evaluations have consistently shown little or no deterrent effects of the program on substance abuse. The program, which is implemented in grades five and six, demonstrates that children who participate in it are as likely to use drugs as those who do not participate. The strength of the program is that it has shown to have positive effects on the children's attitudes toward police.

Researchers cite several reasons for DARE's in effectiveness. Among these are its limited use of social skills training, and it is developmentally inappropriate, coming too early in a child's development—it is difficult to teach children who have not gone through puberty how to deal with the peer pressure they will encounter in middle school.

According to DARE developers, changes are now being made at the national level to address these issues. More social skills training is being added and a modified version of the program is being readied for older students. These particular variations of DARE have yet to be evaluated.

Secondary Prevention Programs

Researchers indicate that secondary prevention programs and strategies to reduce youth violence and drug use are implemented on a selected scale, for children at *enhanced risk of youth violence*, and have the purpose of preventing the onset and reducing the risk of violence. Research also shows that programs that focus on the families of high-risk children are among the most effective in preventing violence. These programs include the following strategies:

TEACHING PARENTS

Parent training on specific child management skills has been shown to lead to clear improvements in children's antisocial behavior (including aggression) and family management practices. Studies of disruptive, aggressive, and hyperactive boys and girls have demonstrated that parent training has resulted in reduced aggressive, antiso-cial, and delinquent behaviors; lower arrest rates; less overall delin-quency; and academic improvement. Five parent training programs were mentioned in the research that have been shown to be promis-ing youth violence prevention programs.

The **Montreal Longitudinal Study** or **Preventive Treatment Program** is a two-year intervention program designed to prevent delin-quency among seven- to nine-year-old boys from low-income fami-lies who have been identified as disruptive. This program is made up of a school-based social skills training component (19 sessions) and parent training (17 sessions). The parent sessions are provided every two weeks during the duration of the program and teach parents to read with their children, monitor and reinforce their children's behav-ior, use effective discipline, and manage family crises. A long-term fol-low-up evaluation (on Canadian boys enrolled in the program) found positive effects on academic achievement and avoidance of gang involvement, drug and alcohol use, and delinquency up to age fifteen.

The **Syracuse Family Development Research Program** concen-trates on parents and children from disadvantaged or impoverished families. Included in this program are weekly home visits and parent training by paraprofessional child development trainers and daycare for five year olds that includes child training focusing on social and cognitive skills and child behavior management.

The **Perry Preschool Program** provides early education to chil-dren ages three and four from families with low socioeconomic status. It is a two-year program designed to provide high-quality early child-hood education and promote the young child's intellectual, social, and physical development. Weekly home visits by teachers and referrals for social services are key ingredients.

Both the Syracuse Family Development Research Program and the Perry Preschool Program have demonstrated long-term effects (up to age nineteen) on delinquency, academic achievement, and other school-related outcomes. Also, the Perry Preschool Program has demonstrated significant reductions in antisocial behavior, serious fights, police contacts, and school dropout rates.

The **Parent Child Development Center Programs** offer a broad-range of services including parent training. This program targets low-income families with children age two months to three years. Parent training focuses on mothers as primary caregivers and concentrates on infant and child development, home management, and family communication and interaction skills. Positive effects from this program have been demonstrated on youth violence, antisocial behaviors, fighting, and mother-child relationships.

The **Parent-Child Interaction Training** program targets low-income parents with preschool children who have at least one behavioral or emotional problem. Parents participate in four to five small-group sessions in which they learn parenting skills related to managing child behavior. Research indicates that this intervention program has been shown to improve family management practices and reduce children's antisocial behaviors, such as aggression and anxiety.

VISITING HOMES

Home visitations are another effective family-based approach to preventing youth violence. In this type of program, a nurse or other professional goes into the home to provide training, counseling, or monitoring to low-income and at-risk mothers. This type of approach has been shown to be successful when implemented before children develop behaviors that put them at risk of violence. Research has shown that home visitation—with or without early childhood education programs—has significant long-term effects on violence, delinquency, and related risk factors. There are several key factors for the degree of effectiveness of these programs: length (only long-term programs have demonstrated consistent effects), delivery (nurses appear to be the most effective home visitors), and timing (the earlier these programs begin, the better).

Prenatal and infancy home visitation by nurses is the only home visitation program that meets the criteria (set forth by the Surgeon General's research team) for a Model youth violence prevention program. It also incorporates all of the characteristics associated with the most effective home visitation programs: it is delivered by nurses, begins early, and is long-term. Home visitations are scheduled from one-week intervals to one-month intervals throughout the two-year intervention. The targeted group is low-income, at-risk pregnant women bearing their first child. The goals of the program include: improved health of the mother and child, creating a social support system around the family, and enhancing the mother's personal development.

MULTIPLE SERVICES

Four multicontextual programs for youth violence prevention have shown positive results by addressing problems in the home, the school, and the community.

The **Yale Child Welfare Project** uses home visitations and day care to deliver parent training and other family and child services. This is a thirty-month program that targets first-born infants of mothers with incomes below the poverty level. Normally a social worker makes the home visits, but a variety of care options are provided: pediatric medical care, psychological services, and early education or day care for children. A ten-year follow-up showed positive effects on parental involvement in the child's education and on antisocial behavior, and discovered a diminished need for remedial and supportive services in the years that followed the program.

Striving Together to Achieve Rewarding Tomorrows (CASA-START), formerly known as the Children At Risk (CAR) program, targets at-risk youths from age eleven to thirteen who live in severely distressed neighborhoods. The curriculum is composed of eight core components: community-enhanced policing, case management of youth and families, criminal/juvenile justice and intervention, family services, after-school and summer activities, educational services, mentoring, and incentives for participation. Evaluations of CASASTART have demonstrated positive effects on the avoidance of gateway drug use, violent crime, and drug sales.

The Families and Schools Together, or the **FAST Track** project, is the most comprehensive of these promising multicontextual interventions. This program combines strategies such as social skills training, parent training, home visitations, academic tutoring, and classroom behavior management techniques. It targets children identified as disruptive in kindergarten and makes an effort to prevent severe, chronic conduct problems by increasing communication and strengthening bonds between the school, home, and child. In this way the child's social, cognitive, and problem-solving skills are improved, as well as peer relationships. There have been short-term positive results of this program on several risk factors associated with youth violence. Long-term follow-up studies now in progress will determine if FAST Track has a significant effect on reducing violence related behaviors and improving academic and social behaviors.

Finally, **The Incredible Years Series** is a curriculum for parents, teachers, and students with the purpose of promoting social competence and preventing, reducing, and treating conduct problems in at-risk children ages three to eight. Trained facilitators use a variety of media and techniques to present this program to encourage problem-solving skills, parental involvement in school and parent competence. The teacher-training component focuses on classroom behavior management. The children's curriculum includes social skills, empathy, anger management, and conflict resolution. Evaluations of this program have demonstrated positive effects on child conduct at home and cognitive problem-solving with peers.

Targeting Academics

Academic programs are effective at improving academic achievement, a weak but important risk factor for late-onset youth violence. Five academic achievement programs were reported as showing promising results.

Compensatory education programs target students at risk of academic failure and provide extra tutoring in reading and mathematics. This program uses cross-age or adult tutoring and pulls students from their regular classes to provide additional academic assistance. A meta-analysis of peer and cross-age tutoring of elementary and middle school students has shown substantial effects on academic achievement for both the tutors and those tutored.

Preventive Intervention is a two-year, school-based behavioral reinforcement program that begins in grade seven and targets students with low academic motivation, family problems, or disciplinary problems. The interventions include behavior monitoring and reinforcement in the classroom and enhanced communication—through meetings and reports to parents—and between teachers, students, and parents about school behavior and attendance.

Educational assistance is one of the major components of the **Quantum Opportunities Program**, a community-based intervention targeting adolescents from families receiving public assistance. Students assigned to this program are matched to a peer group and adult care-giver and receive up to 250 hours of educational services, personal development training, life skills training, career planning, and service opportunities in the community.

Both the Preventive Intervention and the Quantum Opportunities Programs have demonstrated positive effects on academic achievement. Preventive Intervention has been shown to reduce drug use and the risk of having a court record five years after participation.

Thinking Skills

Moral reasoning and problem-solving (thinking skills) are a major component of many of the above programs. Some of these programs have demonstrated lasting, positive effects by reducing police contacts and official school disciplinary action. When used with social problem-solving, studies show significantly lower aggression scores and lower rates of externalizing negative, violent behaviors. The evidence is similar when using a thinking skills approach. Improvements in academic skills and in aggressive problem-solving responses have been demonstrated.

The Surgeon General's report suggests that one reason for the effectiveness of social skills interventions is that they are often more comprehensive in scope than other cognitive-behavioral approaches to preventing youth violence.

Ineffective Secondary Prevention Approaches

Research has shown that several popular prevention approaches used in high-risk populations are ineffective. These include gun buy-back programs, firearms training, and mandatory gun ownership. Also, two community-based strategies for preventing youth violence—redirecting youth behavior and shifting peer group norms—have shown a lack of effectiveness in reducing youth violence.

Because these two types of programs bring high-risk youths together, they have been shown to actually increase the cohesiveness of delinquent peer groups and increase deviant and gang-related delinquent behavior.

Tertiary Prevention:
Violent or Seriously Delinquent Youths

The programs and strategies mentioned in this chapter have been labeled *effective, promising,* or *ineffective (Does Not Work)* for youth who have already demonstrated violent or seriously delinquent behavior. The best information on strategies that are either effective or ineffective in reducing the risk of further violence among these youths comes from meta-analyses. The Surgeon General's report drew heavily on meta-analyses to recommend strategies for youths involved in violent or serious crimes and delinquency.[8] The report reaches two major conclusions: (1) that effective treatment can divert a significant proportion of delinquent and violent youths from future violence and crime, and (2) that there is enormous variability in the effectiveness of different types of programs for seriously delinquent youth. What the research tells us is that the most effective programs reduce the rate of subsequent offending by nearly half (46 percent), compared to controls. Also, it reports that the least effective programs actually increase the rate of subsequent offending by 18 percent.

BEHAVIORAL APPROACHES

Behavioral and skill development interventions, which include social perspective-taking and role-taking, have demonstrated reduced serious delinquent behavior for at least 18 months after treatment. Additional research indicates that multimodel, behavioral, and skills-oriented interventions are more effective than counseling and other less structured approaches.[9] The conclusion has been reached that "in most youth populations—universal, selected, or indicated—behavioral and skills-oriented strategies are among the most effective violence prevention approaches."[10]

FAMILY THERAPY

Family clinical interventions using specific strategies have shown to be effective at preventing violence in delinquent youth and preventing further violence in already violent youths. The marital and family therapy by clinical staff is one such approach. A common thread used in clinical interventions is the focus on changing maladaptive or dysfunctional patterns of family interaction and communication, including negative parenting behaviors. These patterns and behaviors are risk factors for youth violence. Marital and family therapy shows consistent, positive effects on family life, child behavior, family interactions, and delinquency.[11]

Three models of tertiary youth violence prevention programs that use family therapy are the following:

The **Functional Family Therapy (FFT)** targets youth from 11 to 18 years that are at risk of or already demonstrating delinquency, violence, substance use, conduct disorder, oppositional defiant disorder, or disruptive behavior disorder. FFT is a multistep, phasic intervention that includes eight to thirty hours of direct services for youths and their families. The various phases of this program include (1) engagement, to reduce the risk of early dropout, (2) motivation, to change maladaptive beliefs and behaviors, (3) assessment, to clarify interpersonal behavior and relationships, (4) behavior change, including skills training for youths and parents, and (5) generalization, in which individualized casework is used to ensure that new skills are applied to functional family needs. These services have been delivered in a wide variety of settings by a various group of interventionists, including supervised paraprofessionals, trained probation officers, mental health technicians, and mental health professionals. Research has shown that the benefits of FFT include effective treatment of conduct disorder, oppositional defiant disorder, disruptive behavior disorder, and alcohol and other drug abuse disorders. Also, the long-term effects include reductions in the need for more restrictive, costly services and other social services; reductions in the incidence of the original problem being addressed; and reductions in the proportion of youths who eventually enter the adult criminal justice system.

Multi-Systemic Therapy (MST) is an intensive family- and community-based treatment that addresses multiple causes of antisocial behavior. This approach is implemented with individuals, families, peers, the school, or with neighbors. It may include one or more of these contexts of implementation. Its target is families with children in the juvenile justice system who are violent, substance-abusing, or chronic offenders and at high risk of out-of-home placement. Four types of services are offered through a home-based model: strategic family therapy, structural family therapy, behavioral therapy, and behavioral parent training. Delivered over a period of four months with sixty contact hours, the program has demonstrated reductions in long-term rates of re-arrest, reductions in out-of-home placements, improvements in family functioning, and reductions in mental health problems among treated youths, compared to controls.

Multidimensional Treatment Foster Care (MTFC) is a multicontextual clinical intervention designed to target teenagers who have histories of chronic and severe criminal behavior as an alternative to incarceration, groups or residential treatment, or hospitalization.

Research has shown that community-based treatment is more successful than residential treatment. MTFC recruits and trains foster families to offer youths treatment and intensive supervision at home, in school, and in the community. The program offers parent training and other services related to the needs of the family and helps to improve family relationships and reduce delinquency when youths return to their homes. Services include training in behavior management and focused social skills. A community liaison coordinates contacts among case managers and other adult caregivers involved with the youths. Evaluations have shown that this program is able to reduce the number of days of incarceration, overall arrest rates, and drug use, and speed the placement of youths in less restrictive community settings.

Justice system services can be effective for preventing youth violence when they focus on providing services rather than instituting greater penalties. One approach, **wraparound services**, provides comprehensive services tailored to individual youths, as opposed to trying to fit youths into predetermined or inflexible programs. Evaluations have demonstrated a reduction in recidivism and arrests during the year following participation in the program.

One juvenile justice system approach that seems promising is the **Intensive Protective Supervision Project** which removes delinquent youths under the age of sixteen from criminal justice institutions and provides them with proactive and extensive community supervision. This program has been shown to have greater deterrent effects on referrals to juvenile court than standard protective supervision does.

Ineffective Tertiary Programs and Strategies

According to the analysis provided by the Surgeon General's report, several popular programs to prevent further criminal behavior in delinquent youths have been shown to be consistently ineffective. These are boot camps (which focus narrowly on physical discipline), residential programs (which take place in psychiatric or correctional institutions), milieu treatment (a residential program in which the youth resident is involved in decision making and day-to-day interaction for psychotherapeutic discussion), behavior token programs (in which youths are rewarded for conforming to rules, exhibiting prosocial behavior, and not exhibiting antisocial or violent behavior), and waivers to adult court (which approaches the youth as an adult with the premise of "adult time for adult crime"). In all of these programs positive effects on targeted behaviors have been demonstrated while the youths are institutionalized, but such effects disappear when youths leave the program. In the last program, waivers to adult court, evaluations suggest that it increases future criminal behavior rather than deters it, as youths are exposed to more adult, hardened criminals.

There are several counseling, therapy, and social work programs that have also been shown to be ineffective for treating delinquent and violent behavior in youth. Using social casework with individual psychotherapy or counseling with close supervision has failed to produce any positive effects on recidivism. In long-term follow-up analyses, delinquent youths treated in this type of setting show several significant negative effects, including increases in alcoholism, unemployment, marital difficulties, and premature death.[12]

Also, meta-analyses demonstrate that individual counseling can be one of the least effective prevention approaches for delinquent youths. The Surgeon General's analysis concludes, "The effects of this strategy appear to depend largely on the population. Though relatively ineffective for general delinquency and only marginally effective for institutionalized seriously delinquent youths, individual counseling emerged as one of the most effective intervention approaches for non-institutionalized seriously delinquent youths...."[13] Researchers concluded that this study illustrates the importance of program characteristics other than content, particularly the importance of matching the program to the appropriate population."[14]

One tertiary youth violence prevention intervention meets the criteria of "Does not work." This is the Scared Straight program, which relies on shock probation or parole in which brief encounters with inmates describing the brutality of prison life is expected to shock, or deter, youths from committing crimes. Numerous studies of this program, which caught the eye of TV producers in the late 1980s and early 1990s, show that the program does not deter future criminal activities. In some studies, youths who participated in Scared Straight actually had higher rates of re-arrest than youths not involved in this intervention.

The Surgeon General's Conclusions

The researchers presenting the Surgeon General's report concluded, "Numerous programs have demonstrated their effectiveness in reducing risk factors for serious violence. At the same time, there is a pressing need to evaluate more youth violence prevention programs. Of the hundreds of programs currently in use throughout the United States, only six met the criteria for a Model program and twenty-one met the criteria for a Promising program. Of the 266 school-based program modules reviewed … all of which were formally evaluated against a control or comparison group, only ten percent received the highest score for scientific rigor. For most violence, crime, and drug prevention programs now being implemented, there is simply no evidence regarding effectiveness."[15] In Chapter 4, "Measures to Ensure School Safety—Model Programs," the Model programs included in the Surgeon General's report will be presented in some detail.

The Surgeon General's researchers concluded that nearly one half of the most thoroughly evaluated strategies for preventing youth violence are ineffective and a few are even harmful. The most effective youth violence programs have the following characteristics:

- They are targeted appropriately,
- They address several age-appropriate risk and protective factors in different contexts, and
- They include several program components that have demonstrated effectiveness at reducing or preventing youth violence, drug use, or antisocial behaviors. These components include the following:

Quality with which a program is implemented and fidelity to the program's design,
Methods of program delivery,
Characteristics of the youths receiving the intervention,
The setting in which the youths are treated, and
The intensity or duration of the intervention.

Research has shown that implementation is at least as important to a program's success as the characteristics and content of the program itself. Studies of program implementation find that the effectiveness depends on the following principles:[16]

- The project addresses a pressing local problem.
- The project has clearly articulated goals that reflect the needs and desires of the "customer."
- The project has a receptive environment in both the parent organization and the larger system.
- The organization has a leader who is committed to the objectives, values, and implications of the project and who can devise practical strategies to motivate and effect change.
- The project has a director who shares the leader's ideas and values and uses them to guide the implementation process and ongoing operation of the project.
- Practitioners make the project their own rather than being coerced into it; that is, they buy into it, participate in its development, and have incentives to maintain its integrity during the process of change.
- The project has clear lines of authority: there is no ambiguity as to who is in charge.
- The change and its implementation are not complex and sweeping.
- The organization has secure administrators, low staff turnover, and plentiful resources.

The Centers for Disease Control and Prevention's (CDC) *Best Practices of Youth Violence Prevention*[17] suggests that many of the same characteristics help determine the success of violence and delinquency prevention programs in our nation's schools and communities. The CDC highlights the importance of training, monitoring, and supporting the staff that implements a program on the local level. The staff must be knowledgeable and committed to the program's success, experienced with the general strategy being used, knowledgeable about the target community, and capable of managing group dynamics and overcoming resistance. Another key element is maintaining community involvement. Finally, it has been shown that linking a youth violence prevention program to existing strategies and support agencies in the community or school can contribute to success.[18]

D.C. Gottfredson and his colleagues[19] have shown, in a study of more than 1,200 schools throughout the United States, that extensive, high-quality training and supervision, as well as support for the program from the principal of the school, are key elements of success. Schools seem to do better and experience more success with standardized materials and methods, as well as programs that can be incorporated into the regular school program. Local buy-in and initiation of school-based delinquency prevention are important predictors of program success. The CDC recommends monitoring the progress and quality of the program implementation on a local level.

The studies cited by the Surgeon General's report offer valuable guidance on how to implement youth violence prevention programs, how to monitor program fidelity, and how to increase community and agency capacity for implementing these programs. Large scale, systemwide intervention is recommended. Addressing the issues of youth violence prevention will require a major investment of time and resources, but, as the report concludes, "It is the essential next step in the continuing effort to find effective solutions to the problem of youth violence."

For schools and school districts or systems searching for a youth violence program, it should be understood that one size does not fit all. One should download the Surgeon General's entire report from the address listed in endnote 1 for this chapter. The major articles and books used to compile this report should also be read, beginning a complete library for other youth-focused professionals to read and disseminate. It is imperative for the success of the program that all key personnel are knowledgeable and "on the same page" when it comes to understanding the local target population and the strategies and programs needed to bring youth violence to an end. In the next section, additional programs are suggested. These programs may or may not have been scientifically evaluated and recommended. It is up to the local agency to assess its own particular needs and identify program components that meet these needs. If such programs are to work effectively in reducing youth violence and aggression, then they must be evaluated in the short- and long-term. This knowledge should then be shared with the community of professionals of which that school or school district is a part. In this way, we will add to our knowledge and understanding of youth violence prevention and intervention programs, of what works and what does not work.

Addendum: Additional Strategies

Although the Surgeon General's research team put together a thorough report on public school safety, several other well-known organizations have brought together significant contributions to this subject, especially providing information about strategies and programs for reducing and preventing youth violence in and around schools. Among these are the ERIC (Educational Resources Information Center) Review, The Center for Mental Health Knowledge Exchange Network, The Clearinghouse on Urban Education, and the National Center for Educational Statistics. Many other groups provide quality information about youth violence. Chapter 6 in this book will provide a comprehensive list of these centers, associations, and alliances for safe schools with a synopsis of the services they provide. The remainder of this chapter summarizes the strategies recommended by the four groups listed above. For more information about these strategies, the reader should check the endnotes for website addresses where articles can be read in full.

ERIC—School Safety: A Collaborative Effort

The Educational Resources Information Center (ERIC) Review, Volume 7, Issue 1,[20] provides quite a detailed format of information on public school safety. This report is divided into three sections: (1) Understanding School Violence, (2) Preventing School Violence, and (3) Initiatives and Resources. Each of these sections is divided into four to six articles, authored by educational and school safety professionals. Each article in this database is a virtual library of additional websites leading to more information on school safety issues.

Since this chapter is concerned with strategies for reducing and preventing school violence or youth violence, we shall concentrate on section two of ERIC's report: "Preventing School Violence." The writers contributing to this section offer six school safety strategies, all of which are recommended by the Surgeon General's report:

1. Schools should become community learning centers.[21] In this way they are able to extend the traditional school day to include before- and after-school programs. Often, community learning centers are open during the summer as well. By keeping school doors open during nontraditional school hours, schools are able to provide students, parents, and the community with access to valuable educational resources. These centers are also safe havens for children, where after-school learning takes place in buildings removed from the violence, drugs, and lack of supervision that permeates some communities. Consider the following benefits of community learning centers:

> *Public schools are often low-cost, accessible locations in which to extend learning.*
> *They give students the opportunities they need to learn and develop in an enriching, safe, and drug-free setting.*
> *They are well positioned to help younger children meet the America Reads Challenge that all children will read independently and well by the end of the third grade.*
> *They provide extra support and encouragement in mathematics education.*
> *They offer children and youth long-term mentoring opportunities to help them master basic skills while providing enrichment activities that encourage the development of lifelong interests.*
> *Finally, they allow parents to become involved and use their diverse talents and resources, serving as role models for students.*

2. A second strategy for increasing school safety is to perform a systematic assessment of the problem.[22] This assessment should include answers to the following questions:

> *What is the school's policy on weapons and violent behavior?*
> *Are students aware of the policy, and is it consistently enforced?*
> *How is violent behavior supported or discouraged by the school climate and the expectations of the staff and other students?*
> *What attempt is being made to teach students nonviolent conflict resolution?*
> *Are students appropriately supervised?*

Are staff members taught to spot the potential for violent incidents and
to defuse them?
Is there a gang influence in the school?
What role does the principal play in violence reduction?
Can students learn nonviolent behaviors?
Is there a curriculum aimed at teaching children prosocial skills?
Can the school reduce violence by children with serious problems?

3. "Safety by Design"[23] focuses on the design of the school building and other facilities. The purpose is to improve school safety by incorporating certain design elements, such as inconspicuous surveillance features and access-control features in the renovation of existing schools and in the construction of new schools. One safety-by-design approach, Crime Prevention Through Environmental Design, blends effective design with the physical, social, and psychological needs of students, faculty, and staff. Consider the following recommendations:

Promote a sense of ownership in the school campus by dividing the school
buildings into separate areas appropriate for each age group.
Create multiple student-friendly areas where students can gather and
where they are easily monitored.
Promote visual monitoring by maximizing sight lines for school entrances,
hallways, cafeterias, playgrounds, student gathering areas, and other
key locations.
Locate bathrooms in areas that facilitate monitoring.
Provide natural access control by (1) limiting the number of entrances to
and exits from school parking lots and providing for easy closure of
entrances during non-peak hours; (2) eliminating interior or exterior
entrapment areas; defining hallways, classrooms, offices, and school
wings or departments through the use of varied wall and floor colors,
textures, and materials; and (3) directing all visitors through one
entrance that offers contact with a receptionist who controls visitor reg-
istration and distribution of visitor passes.

4. Implement a school-wide behavioral management system.[24] Although school-wide behavioral management systems vary, most have certain features in common. The emphasis is on consistency, both throughout the school and across classrooms. The entire school staff (including cafeteria workers and bus drivers) is expected to adopt strategies that will be uniformly implemented. As a result, the success of the program depends on professional development and the long-term commitment of the school's leadership team. Common features of the school-wide behavioral management system will include the following:

Total staff commitment to managing student behavior.
Clearly defined and communicated expectations and rules.
Clearly stated consequences and procedures for correcting rule-breaking
  behaviors.
An instructional component for teaching students self-control, social skills,
  or both.
A support plan to address the needs of students with chronic challenging
  behaviors.

The keys to such a plan include unified attitudes among school personnel, unified expectations which are consistent and fair, unified consequences for behavioral violations which are applied consistently throughout the school, and unified team roles in which all school personnel have clear responsibilities. From a preventive standpoint, researchers agree that all schools will benefit from having in place a clearly defined, consistently enforced behavioral management system that is designed to support students in controlling their own behaviors.

5. A fifth strategy emphasized by the ERIC Review's "School Safety: A Collaborative Effort," is improving ethnic and racial relations in the school.[25] The report says, "In recent years, several factors have contributed to conflicts among students of different backgrounds: changes triggered by the civil rights movement, the diversity of United States immigrants, and an increasing awareness of ethnic identity. Tensions can exist among different ethnic and racial groups despite the presence of those groups in the United States for generations. Groups' conflicts can affect academic achievement as well as social relationships." The following suggestions are provided for reducing ethnic and racial tensions in schools:

  Identify functions of ethnic and racial conflicts. Researchers have found
    that students in multiethnic schools tend to resegregate themselves for
    social activities and to form friendship cliques. This can lead to ethnic
    and racial conflicts.
  Ethnic boundaries may be important depending on the income and age of
    the students, and the social and economic conditions in their larger soci-
    ety.
  Group conflicts may also create leadership roles for students and make
    group members feel less alienated. The potential for conflict increases in
    proportion to the perceived benefits of membership in the group.
  Consequently, for schools to focus on academics, they must make efforts to
    prevent ethnic and racial clashes. Recognizing common values and dif-
    ferential power (some groups "belong" more than others) is essential for

maintaining stability and positive relationships in multiethnic class-rooms.

Interventions to reduce prejudice and discrimination are also essential. Two methods are recommended: (1) expose students to the contributions of different ethnic groups through drama, films, biographies, novels, and other methods to present members of all groups in a respectful way; and (2) use cooperative learning, mixing students of different ethnicities and races in working groups that receive rewards, recognition, or evaluations based on how much they can improve each member's academic performance. When used correctly, cooperative learning methods can create thoughtful, equitable interactions needed to promote positive racial attitudes, resulting in intergroup friendships, improved inter group attitudes, and academic achievement.

6. Finally, use conflict resolution[26] to allow students to resolve disputes peacefully outside the school's traditional disciplinary procedures. Schools that maintain conflict resolution programs teach, model, and incorporate the processes and problem-solving skills of mediation, negotiation, and collaboration. A fundamental concept of conflict resolution is that the disputing groups or individuals solve the problem themselves. Peer mediation has often been used in conflict resolution programs; however, the Surgeon General's research team found no positive results of this approach and stated that peer mediation often created more problems than it resolved.

A working conflict resolution program can have the following benefits:

Support violence prevention policies by teaching skills and processes for - solving problems before they escalate to violence.

Help students develop personal behavioral management skills, act responsibly in the school community, and accept the consequences of their own behavior.

Help students develop the fundamental competencies (self-control, self-respect, empathy, and teamwork) necessary to make a successful transition to adulthood.

Teach cognitive and other skills necessary for high academic achievement.

Teach students to respect others as individuals and as group members.

Teach students how to build and maintain responsible and productive intergroup relations.

The Conflict Resolution Education Network (CREnet), part of the National Institute for Dispute Resolution, is the primary national and international clearinghouse for information, resources, and technical assistance related to conflict resolution and training. For more information, visit their website at **http://www.crenet.org** or visit http://ojjdp.ncjrs.org, the U.S. Department of Justice's Office of Juvenile Justice and Delinquency Prevention. The U.S. Department of Education's Safe and Drug-Free Schools Program also provides information at http://www.ed.gov/offices/OESE/SDFS.

The Center for Mental Health
Knowledge Exchange Network

The Center for Mental Health Knowledge Exchange Network[27] maintains a website on its School Violence Prevention program. The Center for Mental Health was one of three Federal agencies authorized to design and implement the program, known as the Safe Schools /Healthy Students Initiative. The Model Program, which they have designed, will be presented in Chapter 3 of this book along with other model programs that incorporate the school violence prevention features recommended by the Surgeon General's report.

The Safe Schools/Healthy Students Initiative is a grant program designed to develop real-world knowledge about what works best to reduce school violence. During the first two years of the program, grants of $1 million to $3 million were awarded to 77 local school districts that have formal partnerships with local mental health and law enforcement agencies. Grant awards totaled $145 million. School districts are using these funds to design and implement comprehensive educational, mental health, social service, law enforcement, and juvenile justice services for youth. They are designed to promote healthy childhood development, foster resilience, and prevent youth violence.

The principles of this program include:

- Combining security with healthy childhood development.
- Approaching school violence as a public health issue.
- Offering comprehensive, coordinated services along the path of childhood development.
- Encouraging partnerships among school districts, law enforcement agencies, and local mental health agencies.
- Building resilience to conflict and applying the principles of creative cooperation in human relationships.
- Creating safe and drug free schools.
- Replicating services known to work.

To support the Safe Schools/Healthy Students Initiative, the Center for Mental Health has undertaken a number of other projects, including the development of:

- A national public education campaign to generate a broad range of communications products and activities to enhance awareness, understanding, and application of strategies for preventing school violence and developing healthy children.
- A national coordinating center to provide training and technical assistance for Safe Schools/Healthy Students grantees and for applicants of the program who did not receive awards.
- Interactive computer learning software to assist students, parents, and teachers in developing positive attitudes, adequate knowledge, and effective skills for preventing school violence.
- A grant program targeted at community-based organizations to build community consensus and collaboration and to pilot an evidence-based program that promotes healthy child development and prevents violence.
- A grant program targeted at state and local government organizations to promote mental health and prevent violence and substance abuse among youth. This program supports the development of self-sustaining coalitions between state and local governments that have community service delivery systems, in order to promote a community-wide understanding of youth problem behaviors and approaches to violence prevention.

The ERIC Clearinghouse on Urban Education

The ERIC Clearinghouse on Urban Education[28] has provided a document written by Wendy Schwartz which overviews many strategies to reduce school violence. The report observes that despite the inconsistencies between school policies and practices, "many promising types of anti-violence strategies, focusing on both discipline and social and personal transformation, have been devised by government, communities, and schools." The report recommends the following:

- Government initiatives, at all levels, to reduce the availability of guns to minors. The 1994 Gun-Free Schools Act mandates a one-year expulsion for students who bring weapons to school. Federal action also includes anti-gang programs and other very focused prevention education.

- Community initiatives that focus on breaking family cycles of violence. These include long-term interventions providing a full range of family services—social services, public housing, and health care. Community initiatives also involve law enforcement, religious and recreational organizations, the schools, and the business community. These involve out-of-school programs to keep youth constructively engaged when their families are unavailable, and provide youth with attention from caring adults and good role models. Helping youth find employment is another important way for communities to reduce property crime and help build adolescents' self-esteem and sense of responsibility. It gives youth people a sense of "future" and hope for a better tomorrow.

- School improvement that will increase a student's engagement, attendance, and performance. School reform programs, especially those requiring strong family involvement, report increased attendance and student satisfaction. Schools can reduce violence by promoting mutual respect among all members of their community, student self-respect, and appreciation for diversity. Schools demonstrate respect for students through availability of good facilities and resources, and provides a perception of safety—schools in urban areas, where violence can be a particular problem, are among the most overcrowded and poorly equipped and maintained.

- School safety policies demonstrate a commitment to violence prevention and helps staff and students feel safe. These include, among other things, a zero tolerance for guns and other types of violent offenses. They may include dress regulations.

- Prevention strategies will include school security—student monitoring by teachers and security officers—and teacher involvement. Also, training in violence prevention for all staff members will make the school safer and help the staff feel more secure. Programs should include the development of the ability to identify students at risk of anti-social behavior for preventive intervention, to identify and diffuse potential violence, and to deal safely with violence should it erupt. Training should also include conflict resolution, informal counseling, and knowing when to refer students for additional, specific help. Additional training (on an ongoing basis) should include age-appropriate training in self-esteem development and stress management and reduction, anger management, impulse control, appreciation of diversity, mediation, and anti-gang measures.

The report concludes, "Concern about increasing youth violence is being channeled into a variety of innovative, and potentially effective, programs around the country." Elements of these programs vary with the needs of each community, but the most effective ones:

1. Make an accurate assessment of the existence of violence and, especially, gang activity.
2. Use all the resources in the community, including social service and law enforcement, and not just rely on school officials to deal with the problem.
3. Incorporate family services into both community and school programs.
4. Intervene early in a child's life.
5. Include not only anti-violence strategies but also positive experiences.
6. Create and communicate clearly defined behavior codes, and enforce them strictly and uniformly.
7. Prepare to engage in a long-term effort.

National Center for Educational Statistics

The National Center for Educational Statistics[29] has prepared yearly reports on "Violence Prevention Programs." The report prepared for 1996–1997 was of particular interest because of the violence prevention strategies that it recommends. Consider the following:

A majority of public school principals (78 percent) reported having some type of formal school violence prevention or reduction programs. The percentage of schools with both 1-day and ongoing programs (43 percent) was almost double the percentage of schools with only ongoing programs (24 percent) and quadruple the percentage of schools with only 1-day programs (11 percent). Schools in which a serious crime was reported were more likely to have violence prevention programs than those in which no crime or only less serious crimes had occurred (93 percent compared with 74 and 79 percent, respectively. Schools with serious crime also had more programs per school. They reported a mean of 6 programs per school compared with 3.4 violence prevention programs in schools with no crime or lesser crimes only.

In some public schools, incidents during 1996–97 requiring police contact were used to modify or introduce new violence prevention programs. Of schools with violence prevention programs that had reported one or more crimes in 1996–97, 31 percent had used these incidents to introduce or modify their violence prevention programs. School principals were asked if, during the 1996–97 school year, they had any formal programs or efforts intended to prevent or reduce school violence. Selected components of prevention or reduction programs were listed and principals were asked if any of their programs included each of the following:

- Prevention curriculum, instruction, or training for students, such as social skills training.
- Behavioral programming or behavior modification for students.
- Counseling, social work, psychological, or therapeutic activity for students.
- Activities involving individual attention for students, such as tutoring and mentoring.
- Recreational, enrichment, or leisure activities for students.
- Student involvement in resolving student conduct problems, such as dispute or conflict resolution or mediation, and student court.
- Training, supervision, or technical assistance in classroom management for teachers.
- Review, revision, or monitoring of school-wide discipline practices and procedures.
- Community or parent involvement in school violence prevention programs or efforts.
- Reorganization of school, grades, or schedules, such as school within a school, "houses," or "teams" of students.

The prevention curriculum, counseling and social work, and

review and revision of school-wide discipline practices were components used most often by schools with violence prevention or reduction programs (89 percent, 87 percent, and 85 percent, respectively), while reorganization of school, grades, or schedules was used least often (28 percent). With the exception of community and parental involvement, which 48 percent of schools reported using, between 63 percent and 81 percent of the schools with violence prevention or reduction programs reported using the remaining components.

Conclusions

What has been discovered from reviewing the Surgeon General's report and the reports outlined in the addendum to this chapter is a consistency of research, component-recommendations for school violence prevention programs, and a recommendation to evaluate the programs and strategies in use in your school or school district—if possible, by comparing with a control group. In the next chapter, "Measures to Ensure School Safety—Model Programs," several model programs will be outlined which incorporate the strategies and measures included in this chapter's recommendations. Our purpose is quite straightforward and simple: in Chapter 1 we focused on the causes of school violence, in Chapter 2 on government involvement from both the federal and state levels, and in this chapter, on the strategies—produced by careful research and evaluation—that make up a model program. The next chapter will seek out model programs that have basically followed the prescriptions laid down by these strategies.

No one school district or individual school will include all of these strategies in its program. Each program will reflect the particular needs and problems of the school community. Obviously, an urban school's program will be different than a rural school's program. Even a district program, albeit with a consistent focus and intent, will vary from school to school because of both school and community variances. This book has been prepared to provide the principal and central office violence prevention liaison a directional tool for finding additional resources and information to support the school and school district's violence prevention efforts. By checking the websites listed in this chapter, the administrator will discover additional resources in each article (see bibliographies for each selection). Here the professional educator will find research and additional information on violence prevention education that covers most conceivable situations. Spending some time with these resources will pay huge dividends in the development of your school or school district violence prevention program.

4

Measures to Ensure School Safety: Model Programs

The United States Department of Education has reported that the public's concern about violence in schools has been manifested in media stories, Congressional testimony, and numerous studies and reports that vividly underscore the pervasiveness of the problem. Nowhere, however, is the magnitude of the nation's concern about school violence reflected more urgently than in Goal 7 of the Goals 2000: Educate America Act, adopted by Congress and signed into law by President Clinton in March 1994. Goal 7 states, "By the year 2000, every school in America will be free of drugs and violence and will offer a disciplined environment conducive to learning." The supporting narrative for this goal states that "no child or youth should be fearful on the way to school, be afraid while there, or have to cope with pressures to make unhealthy choices."[1]

This chapter addresses seriously the public's concern about discipline and violence in America's schools. Youth violence is worse than it has ever been and is on the rise. It permeates every component of American society. Recognizing the seriousness of this problem is important, but one must also say that the vast majority of our youth are not violent, nor have they committed acts of violence. There are three groups of students in a school (what is called the 80-15-5 rule). Eighty percent rarely break rules or violate principles. Fifteen percent break the rules on a somewhat regular basis by refusing to accept classroom principles and restrictions. If not clearly apprised of expectations and consequences of their behavior, these students can disrupt learning for all the other students. The last five percent of the students are chronic rule breakers and are generally out of control most of the time. They may also commit acts of violence in the school and in the community.

Therefore, it is understandable that school administrators want the best information available that enables them to construct anti-violent programs that work for them. Not all of the strategies mentioned in Chapter 3, nor the model programs that will be outlined in this chapter, will fit every school or every occasion of youth violence prevention. They are presented here as resources for adapting to the school and community, recognizing that each learning community will have different characteristics and, therefore, different needs. If you find one of these programs that fits your school or classroom, the full text of the source should be read and discussed with faculty and parents.

Preventing Violence in Schools

Mary Hatwood Futrell and Lee Etta Powell comment, "Youth violence in many schools, frequently mirroring the situation in the surrounding community, has reached pandemic proportions. In some communities the situation is so bad that young offenders are being sent to boot camps or 'shock incarceration programs,' or are required to perform supervised community service." They continue, "Especially frightening is the increased availability of weapons, guns in particular. The fact that more and more weapons are showing up in schools underscores how readily accessible they are. In response to this phenomenon, schools are resorting to random checks of students' book bags, backpacks, or lockers. They are also increasing their use of metal detectors to identify students carrying weapons. Many schools are moving to physical means of control-fences, blocked access roads, and locked and chained doors to guard against violence."

Futrell and Powell have authored a thorough research study, "Preventing Violence in Schools."[2] This study provides an overview of the factors contributing to school violence—the locations where much of school violence occurs, a profile of school violence perpetrators, the most likely victims of school violence, how violence impedes education, and measures to ensure school safety. Their section on school-wide strategies and long-term solutions constitute a "model" program if followed and adapted by teachers and administrators. This material is a revision of an earlier manuscript and, as they comment, offers "some recommendations based upon our reflections as teachers—who taught for 15 and 10 years, respectively, in urban centers—and as concerned citizens, about what schools and communities can do to stem the tide of violence in schools, and, hopefully, in society in general.... All of the strategies described herein are important and, perhaps, necessary. However, they are too little and, perhaps, too late. Most strategies to curb violence in school and society are designed to respond to violence after it has occurred rather than to prevent it."

School-Wide Strategies

Monitoring Student Behavior and Movement. The most common school security measure used to prevent violence or other disruptive acts requires school staff, in particular teachers and security staff, to monitor students' movements in and around the school. Thus, staff monitor hallways, doorways, restrooms, the cafeteria or lunchrooms, and the areas of the campus where students tend to congregate. In addition, more and more school funds are used to hire retired police officers or security guards to patrol buildings and provide security at sports and other school sponsored events. Equally effective, if not more so, and less costly than guards, is the use of students' parents as monitors and teachers' aides. Youth are less likely to misbehave or engage in violent acts if parents from their neighborhood are highly visible on a daily basis in their school. Several schools have used this strategy and found it to be highly effective.

Discipline and Dress Codes. Institutionalization of discipline and dress codes is another strategy used to curb violence. Administrators, teachers, parents, and students should develop these codes collaboratively. The school district's legal staff, to assure compliance with state school law, should review discipline and dress codes. Equally important, schools must be sure that the rules created have a purpose and that they explicitly tell students what kinds of behavior are acceptable. Included in these codes should be policies that delineate how the school will deal with students who are chronic disciplinary problems, such as suspensions, expulsions, and filing criminal charges against perpetrators if necessary.

Discipline and dress codes should be reviewed and revised to ensure that they are appropriate for the student population and that they are contributing to a safe, orderly school environment. Every administrator, teacher, parent, and student should receive a copy of the codes. They should be reviewed in each class so that every student is aware of their existence and the consequences of violating any rules. School administrators and teachers should ensure that the codes are implemented consistently and firmly, but also fairly.

To assure that parents receive and review the school's discipline code, the State of Virginia enacted a law effective May 1995 requiring parents, under penalty of a fine, to sign and return a copy of the school rules. The law also requires parents of suspended students to meet with school officials or face a fine up of to five hundred dollars. Similarly, a 1994 Alabama law holds parents liable when students damage school property. The intent of these laws is to make parents "more accountable for the misbehavior of their sons and daughters."

Counseling Programs. Schools should establish counseling programs for students, and assure that students do indeed have access to their counselors. Currently, most elementary schools do not have counselors, and if they do, they are in the schools for only one or two days per week. At the high school level, counselors are part of the staff. However, the average high school counselor has between 350 and 400 students to advise. Needless to say, students are lucky to see their counselor once during a school year—usually when it is time to sign up for the next year's classes—and this contact often occurs in a large group. In order to effectively counsel the students in the school—whether academically or behaviorally—and to ensure that students have access to their assigned counselor on a regular basis, counselors should be assigned no more than 125–150 students per school year. They should be relieved of clerical and other non-counseling responsibilities.

Conflict Resolution Programs. Another form of "counseling" is the widespread use of conflict resolution strategies to defuse potentially violent situations and to persuade those involved to use nonviolent means to resolve their differences. It has been observed that conflict, with its roots in competition, poor communication, and miscalculation, is a normal part of life and cannot be eliminated (whether in schools [public or private] or the community at large). It is extremely important to violence prevention that we change how we respond to conflict.

Schools that have adopted conflict resolution strategies are trying to teach young people new ways of channeling their anger into constructive, nonviolent responses to conflict. As a means of addressing violence, conflict resolution programs in schools start by identifying a core group of student leaders in the school. This group receives intensive training and supervision in the use of conflict resolution strategies and student mediation. Members of the "conflict resolution team" then use their skills and knowledge to help maintain order in the school by counseling their peers, intervening in disputes among students, helping them talk through their problems, and training other students to use conflict resolution strategies. Conflict resolution strategies should be used in individual classrooms as well as school-wide. In addition, high school team members should visit students in elementary school and teach them the value of conflict resolution skills. Thus, conflict resolution strategies can be used for both prevention and intervention.

Crisis Centers. Schools should strongly consider the establishment of crisis centers for students who commit violent acts or threaten violence. Teachers and administrators can refer students to the centers, which should be staffed by professionals who are specially trained to work with violent students. Crisis centers should not be used for long-term interventions, but rather as in-school areas where students can be sent to "cool off" and to receive on-the-spot counseling. Nor should crisis centers be viewed as a replacement for after-school detention programs.

Teacher Crisis Meetings. Efforts to prevent violence in schools must involve teachers at every step of the process. Whether or not told through formal communications channels, all teachers are aware of the discipline problems, including acts of violence, which occur in their school. Strategies designed to eliminate or reduce such problems will not work unless teachers are involved in the design and implementation of programs to establish a safe, orderly environment in the school. Further, it is important for teachers to be part of ongoing discussions regarding the status of discipline problems and acts of violence occurring on the school campus. It is also important for teachers to be able to discuss major discipline problems they are having with students in their classrooms. These discussions can be part of regular monthly faculty meetings or special sessions designed to apprise faculty and staff of any major problems related to violence in the school. When faculty members are aware of what is going on in the school and of strategies to address problems, they are more apt to become actively involved in supporting school-wide efforts to correct the problem. Furthermore, when teachers are part of the process, they are more willing to become part of the school team and to work to achieve the goal of creating a school that is safe for all.

Teacher Team Meetings. Teachers in schools organized into interdisciplinary teams that teach the same group of students can exchange ideas about successful strategies for working with disruptive or violence-prone students during their team meetings. They can learn from each other how best to manage the students' behavior and can establish a uniform set of standards or rules of discipline for their classes to be recognized and supported by the school administration.

Support for Teachers. Critical to the elimination of violent acts in schools is support for teachers' efforts to address discipline problems. Since teachers are the front line school staff members responsible for handling discipline problems, it is paramount that they receive support from their administration. While one of the major complaints from administrators is that teachers are not consistent in applying school discipline rules, teachers often complain that they do not receive support from school administrators when they report students for disruptive, or even violent, behavior. Obviously, teachers must be consistent in applying rules of discipline. And, administrators must provide teachers and other school staff with the assurance that violent students will be dealt with swiftly and firmly, and that teachers will receive support in their efforts to maintain an orderly classroom. Nothing is more discouraging to a teacher than sending a student who is disrupting a classroom to the office, only to see the student return half an hour later to tell friends that his or her misbehavior was not punished. Teachers have to know that they have the total support of the school administration and board of education in their efforts to handle unruly students.

Extended School Hours (community schools). Another strategy being used by an increasing number of schools is extending the number of hours that the school is open to students. In some communities, after the regular school day has ended, schools are kept open so that students can participate in organized activities such as sports, gymnastics, crafts, art, music, tutorial programs, or other activities. Other schools, especially elementary schools, provide space for child-care programs to accommodate working parents who are unable to pick up their children at the end of the school day and do not want them home alone. A trained staff should supervise all of these activities.

Classes for Parents. There is an increasing number of teenage parents who lack social or parenting skills, but are raising children who soon will enter school to begin their own formal education. Often these parents have left school without a high school diploma, thereby limiting their employability. As these young parents are living out their own adolescence, their offspring can experience a benign type of abuse in the form of inadequate nurturing during their early years, lack of attention to their developmental needs, and neglect. Having been victims of abuse and violence, these children tend to grow up to become abusers as adults, thus repeating the cycle of abuse and violence. To serve this population, many school districts have established classes for parents to teach them effective parenting skills, provide them with an opportunity to earn a GED, and offer them vocational training so they can find employment. By participating in such programs, young parents can then provide better guidance to their own children and become a positive role model for them.

Additional Strategies. Since school personnel are faced with competing demands that overcrowd their schedule, acts of disruption are typically handled in a routine manner, following a prescribed discipline code. These codes tend to be legalistic and punitive, and are unlikely to result in sustained improvement in student behavior. Therefore, it can be very useful for schools to also use positive incentives to prevent violence. For example, a successful program in elementary schools called **Getting Caught Being Good** provides a positive approach to curbing students' disruptive and violent behavior. The school establishes a recognition and reward system for students who are observed in a significant act of good school citizenship. The overall goal of this program is to bring about a change in the students and in the school climate so that normative behavior is constructive. Another positive approach to violence prevention is providing students with positive role models. Schools should invite high profile leaders in the community (i.e., police officers, athletes, media representatives, and parents) to visit schools and talk with students about crime and violence.

These strategies indicate that the best school-based violence prevention programs seek to do more than reach students who may be prone to violence and their victims. The most effective programs are designed to change the total school environment by creating a safe school community that believes in and practices nonviolence in resolving differences.

Classroom Strategies

To maintain a safe and orderly classroom conducive to teaching and learning, a teacher must set forth both academic and behavioral expectations for all students. In addition to school-wide codes, each teacher must articulate to students on the first day of class the basic standards of behavior for the class. Additional standards may be developed with input from the students to reinforce their commitment to the standards.

Behavior Standards. The classroom behavior standards should comply with the school's code, but they need not be as detailed. The standards should be given to the students in writing and should be posted in the classroom. They should be clearly stated and understood by all students in the class. Also, a copy of the standards should be sent home to parents. Teachers are responsible for establishing and maintaining the climate in the classroom and for managing the students. It is very important for them to establish control on the first day of school and maintain it steadily thereafter. Students are perceptive and become quickly aware of teachers who are "not in control" of their classrooms. Being in control does not mean being rigid or being a "tyrant"; it means asserting authority and demanding and getting respect.

Teachers also must ensure that the behavior standards are followed, and they must do so in a manner that is fair, but firm and consistent. Students who fail to comply with the discipline standards must be dealt with quickly and firmly. Constantly changing the rules or extending the list will simply cause confusion. Failure to enforce them will result in the students' ignoring or constantly breaking them; it will lead to chaos.

Academic Expectations. Equally important, and often a factor ignored in discussions about discipline and violence in schools, is the academic side of the issue. Again, it is the responsibility of the teacher to establish the ethos in the classroom regarding academic expectations. The objectives for each lesson, and each unit, should be clearly articulated to the students prior to teaching it. Preferably, these objectives should be in writing, either on the chalkboard or on paper given to the students. They should be explained to the class along with an explanation of the teaching and learning activities to be used to achieve them.

Classrooms where the academic objectives are unclear are fertile for disruptive student behavior, and, perhaps, violence. This does not mean that every student should be seated quietly at a desk with a book open or busy filling in the blanks on a form. It does mean that the lessons have been carefully planned to elicit maximum teaching and learning. It means students are actively engaged in learning activities—sometimes in groups, at other times working alone, and later as a full class. It means using strategies to ensure that students comprehend what is being taught and are able to demonstrate their understanding of the coursework. It means insisting that all students strive to meet the academic as well as behavioral standards for the class and assisting those who have difficulty doing so.

Teachers know that disruptive or violent behavior in the classroom is a way for some students to mask their frustration and anger over their academic deficiencies. The fact that all students are not alike and do not acquire knowledge the same way must be reflected in the teacher's method of instruction. Applied strategies of effective teaching, along with lesson plans that respond to students' cultural diversity and learning styles, can significantly reduce instances of potentially disruptive or violent behavior.

Strategies for Individual Students

Futrell and Powell have focused on violence in schools and strategies for addressing the problem from a classroom or school-wide perspective. It is also important to focus on individual students in order to prevent them from becoming chronically disruptive or violent. The following strategies are designed to encourage students to focus on discipline as a positive means of behavior.

Tutors and Mentors. The discussion above cited lack of parental supervision at home as one of the factors contributing to student violence. With the absence of a "significant adult" in their lives, many students lack the nurturing that comes from parental support and guidance. Some school communities seek to fill this void by establishing tutoring programs and providing mentors for students. The mentors are community volunteers from business, service organizations, colleges and universities, churches, and retiree organizations. They have made a significant difference in the lives of many young people.

Employment. It has been observed that some schools and communities have made efforts to reduce the number of property crimes by providing part-time employment for students during the school year and full-time employment during the summer months. The goals of these work programs include building self-esteem and a sense of responsibility, and learning the value of money and the importance of getting a good education and staying in school until graduation.

Youth Collaboratives. With encouragement and financial support for pilot programs from the National Alliance of Business and the Ford Foundation, several urban school districts have organized "youth collaboratives."[6] These collaboratives, also known as **The Compact Project,** began with the Boston Compact and have extended to over a dozen large urban school districts. Focusing initially on school dropout prevention and the preparation of youth for the work force, they were among the early proponents of the need to provide coordinated services for youth and families. With the support of the business community, school districts seek to address the needs of students at risk of educational failure through the combined efforts of the city government, health, law enforcement, education, and social service agencies, and the religious community.

Long-Term Solutions

Some would say that the best way to address the issue of violence in schools is to simply get tougher with the perpetrators. Others say that the solution must be to instill better moral values, for children are suffering from ethical confusion and media pollution. Still others would say that the solution is to attack violence at its roots through a variety of efforts, such as providing parents with training in parenting skills, providing the whole family with social and economic supports and training in nonviolent conflict resolution, and providing children with a strong sense of right and wrong and a safe community in which to develop. Taken alone, each solution is too simplistic. Taken together, the three options make a strong program for stemming youth violence in schools and in communities.

Recognizing and accepting the need for change are critical steps toward any efforts to reduce violence in schools. Change is a process that requires a sustained commitment from those desiring it—individuals, families, schools, and communities. Working to increase discipline, order, and safety in schools requires all parties to examine the attitudes, behaviors, and values that define them. Finally, but most importantly, youths themselves must learn that they are responsible for their behavior and actions, and that they are personally accountable for what they do in school and in the community.

Early Intervention. It is at the formative level of a child's life (until approximately year nine) that families and communities must inculcate positive attitudes and modes of behavior. Therefore, at the pre-kindergarten through fourth grade levels, school districts should implement counseling programs, role modeling and mentoring, and antiviolence and safety programs for students. This agenda must also include developing respect for oneself and others. Forums should be provided, for example, where students can discuss sensitive issues related to racism, poverty, sexism, religion, and violence.

In addition, conflict resolution programs should be integrated into the school's curriculum and participation should be required for all students. These programs should be introduced early and resources should be committed to sustain them at all levels of the school system. Such programs should also be accessible to parents who wish to participate in them.

District-Wide Discipline Codes. Every school district should have a clearly defined discipline code that is communicated to students and their parents each year. A major focus of it should be recognizing discipline as a positive rather than a negative sense of being. The emphasis must be on prevention as well as intervention. Equally important, the discipline code should be enforced consistently, firmly, and fairly.

It is also critical for teachers, parents, and members of student services programs to work together to help schools and communities address the issue of increased youth violence. School psychologists, counselors, nurses, social workers, speech-language pathologists, and all other student services personnel must be part of the violence prevention decision-making process. Further, schools should maintain a liaison with local police authorities since some acts of violence in schools are a spillover from disputes that originate in the community.

Health and Social Services. Students experiencing emotional, psychological, or physical problems that interfere with learning should have access to the educational, therapeutic, counseling, and diagnostic services to correct those problems. Parents who need support and training to be better parents should have access to programs that provide it. It is particularly important where there is evidence of child abuse or neglect. These programs are also important for families with nonexistent or poor communication between parents and their children. Children with disabilities should be provided with the special education and related services that they need—not just because it is the law, but because it is the right thing to do.

Staff Training. Teachers see the negative and positive sides of student behavior and attitudes long before school boards, central administrators, or the community become alarmed and decide to act. They know the symptoms of incipient violence long before the metal detectors, security guards, or random searches become part of the school environment. Teachers see signs of disruptive, even violent, behavior as early as preschool and elementary school.

Yet, teachers are often unprepared to address the needs of disruptive, often violent, youth. Therefore, teachers and building-level administrators must receive intensive training and sustained staff development for dealing with violence. At the same time, teachers and their professional organizations, student services personnel, school district officials, and community leaders must work together to develop programs to reduce and prevent violence in schools. These programs must include strategies for working with families and community groups because schools cannot do the job alone. In addition, school districts should inform teachers and administrators about social services available in the community and how they can be accessed.

Unfortunately, teachers often do not know how best to help young people who are having problems. Thus, teacher and administrator preparation programs in schools of education must include the following types of training, with master teachers, if possible: how to create and maintain a well-managed and well-organized classroom, how to deal with student disruptions, how to work effectively with parents so that their children meet academic and behavioral expectations, how to work effectively with an ethnically and economically diverse student body, and how to find community health and social services and link families to them.

Community Programs. Students must also have experiences in their homes and communities that reinforce positive attitudes and behaviors. Religious groups, the media, civic organizations, and student groups, such as Girls and Boys Clubs, should provide continuing opportunities and experiences that enable students to resolve differences or conflicts nonviolently. Central to these efforts must be parents and guardians. They, in particular, must assume a greater responsibility for their sons' and daughters' behavior within the home, the school, and the community.

U.S. Department of Education and U.S. Department of Justice "Model Programs"

The U. S. Department of Justice has identified a number of model school safety programs and strategies.[3] Many of these strategies were outlined in Chapter 3 of this book. What follows is a sample of the model school safety programs that the Department of Justice has identified under a grant to the Hamilton Fish National Institute on School and Community Violence, with the assistance of the Vanderbilt Institute for Public Policy. The models in highlighted in this section were randomly selected by the ERIC Review's "School Safety: A Collaborative Effort," from twelve programs listed in the Model Programs section of the *Annual Report on School Safety, 1998* under the categories Aggression/Fighting and Bullying.

Important to school administrators seeking programs and strategies in school safety that work, the Department of Justice has designated these as either "demonstrated" or "promising." Demonstrated models are those that have been rigorously tested in the field and have solid evidence of their effectiveness. Promising models are those that are well designed but have yet to be thoroughly tested. Local schools and school district administrators should keep in mind that the selection of a program should be based on their own thorough assessment of specific school and community needs. The design of the local assessment should necessarily get input from community leaders, organizations, and parents.

Aggression and Fighting

A *demonstrated model* for middle schools is the **Anger Coping Program** for selected male students. A school counselor and mental health counselor hold 18 weekly small-group sessions during the school day. The lessons emphasize self-management and self-monitoring, understanding the other's point of view, and social problem-solving skills. Evaluations show that aggressive boys who have completed the Anger Coping Program have been found to have lower rates of drug and alcohol involvement, higher levels of self-esteem, and stronger problem-solving skills than those who have not completed the program. For more information contact John E. Lochman, Ph.D., The University of Alabama Department of Psychology, Box 870348, Tuscaloosa, Alabama 35487; Phone: 205-348-5083; Fax: 205-348-8648; E-mail: jlochman@gp.as.ua.edu.

Another program, **Positive Adolescent Choices Training (PACT)**, for middle and high schools, is also a *demonstrated model*. It has been developed for high-risk African-American youth and other high-risk youth selected by teachers for conduct problems or histories of victimization. Methods used in this program include videotaped vignettes and role-playing where students learn social skills such as giving and accepting positive and negative feedback, negotiating, problem-solving, and resisting peer pressure. Evaluations demonstrate that rates of physical aggression at school and violence-related court charges are fifty percent lower among those students who have completed the PACT program compared with those who have not.

For more information about this program, contact Betty R. Yung, Ph.D., Director, Center for Child and Adolescent Violence Prevention, Wright State University, School of Professional Psychology, Ellis Human Development Institute, 9 North Edwin C. Moses Boulevard, Dayton, Ohio 45407; Phone 937-775-4300; Fax: 937-775-4323; E-mail: betty.yung@wright.edu.

For grades K–5, **PeaceBuilders** is a *demonstrated model* for students of mixed ethnicity that has been evaluated in urban and suburban elementary schools. PeaceBuilders seeks to change "a way of life" and should not be thought of as just another program. Its focus is to change the characteristics of the school setting that trigger aggressive, hostile behavior. This program seeks to increase the availability of prosocial models to enhance social competence and decrease the frequency and intensity of aggressive behavior. Researchers discovered that this program improved students' social competence, especially when students had two years of exposure to the program, and curtailed expected increases in students' aggressive behavior. For more information, contact Jane Gulibon, Heartsprings, Inc., P. O. Box 12158, Tucson, Arizona 85732; 1-800-368-9356; Phone: 520-322-9977; Fax: 520-322-9983; E-mail: custrel@heartsprings.org; or check their Web site at http://www.peacebuilders.com.

Bullying

A comprehensive *promising model* is **Bully Proofing Your School** for elementary students. The components include staff involvement in deciding how to reduce bullying; a student curriculum using role playing, modeling, and class discussions; victim support that emphasizes enhancing self-esteem and social skills; an intervention for bullies that teachers anger control and empathy; and interaction with the parents of bullies and victims. The purpose of the program is to shift power away from bullies, not on punishing them. No evaluation data are available. For additional information, contact Sally Stoker; Phone: 303-743-3670, ext. 8317.

The Bullying Prevention Project, for elementary and middle schools, is also a *promising model* that includes the following:

- Assistance to school staff and parents in identifying and handling bullies and their victims,
- Classroom activities, such as role playing and creative writing, that generates discussions of bullying, and
- School-wide anti-bullying activities, including reinforcement of positive behavior, school-wide behavioral rules, and sanctions for bullying.

A preliminary evaluation of this program found promising results and the program continues to be enhanced and tested. *The Blueprint on the Bullying Prevention Program* is available for $10 from the Center for the Study and Prevention of Violence, at 303-492-8465. Contact Susan P. Limber, Project Director, Bullying Prevention Project, Institute on Family and Neighborhood Life, 243 Poole Agricultural Center, Clemson University, Clemson, South Carolina 29634-5205; E-mail: slimber@clemson.edu.

For more information about violence prevention programs, contact the U. S. Department of Education and the U. S. Department of Justice. In particular, see the *Annual Report on School Safety, 1998*. This report can be found online at http://www.ed.gov/pubs/AnnSchool-Rept98. The 1999 *Annual Report on School Safety* can be found at http://www.ed.gov/offices/OESE/SDFS/news.html.

The 1999 Report complements, but does not replace, the 1998 Report. Paper copies of both reports can be ordered from the U. S. Department of Education's Publication Center (ED Pubs) by calling toll free 1-877-433-7827. This report comes from the Expert Panel on Safe, Disciplined, and Drug-free Schools convened by the U. S. Department of Education in the year 2000. In addition to these reports and information about model programs, contact the following: http://www.ed.gov/offices/OERI/ORAD/KAD/expert_panel/drug-free.html.

U. S. Department of Education and U. S. Department of Justice "Putting It All together: An Action Plan"

The model programs in this chapter highlight the importance of school safety in the lives of children and teachers. The U. S. Department of Education and U. S. Department of Justice have summarized the steps that parents, educators, business and community leaders, and students can take to make their schools safer.[4] From the 1998 *Annual Report on School Safety,* we are able to generate the following action plan for implementing a safety plan in your school and school district:

Parents

- Take an active role in your children's education. Make sure that your children do their homework and attend class. Get to know teachers and administrators by attending school functions and showing up for important parent-orientation meetings.
- Listen to and talk with your children regularly, because everyday conversations create opportunities to teach children social, problem solving, and anger management skills.
- Act as role models. Settle your own conflicts peacefully, and manage your own anger without violence.
- Establish clear rules of behavior, and discipline your children consistently. Discuss behaviors, punishment, and rewards with your children.
- Make it clear to your children that you support school policies and that you do not tolerate violent behavior.
- Discourage your children from name-calling, teasing, and other forms of bullying.
- Keep guns and other weapons out of reach of unsupervised children. Ensure that firearms are locked away, well secured, and stored separately from ammunition.
- Insist on knowing your children's friends, whereabouts, and activities.
- Work with other parents to develop standards for school-related events and activities, and ensure that there is adult supervision at these events and activities.
- Join with other parents through school, neighborhood, civic, or religious organizations to talk about concerns regarding youth and violence in your community.

Educators

- Assess the school's security needs. Enlist school security professionals in designing and maintaining a school security system.
- Implement school-wide education and training on safety and violence prevention.
- Actively involve students in making decisions about school policies and programs.
- Design and consistently enforce a clear, effective discipline policy and other school policies that support and reward prosocial behavior.
- Devise a system for reporting and analyzing incidents that violate school policies.
- Monitor the school to ensure that it is clean and safe.
- Create a climate of tolerance. Ensure that all students are respected and treated equally, regardless of ethnicity, race, religion, sex, socioeconomic status, or other characteristics.
- Provide appropriate educational and crisis-response services to all students, including access to school psychologists and counselors.

- Use alternative schools to educate violent students.
- Prepare an annual report on school crime and safety, and distribute it to school staff, parents, students, and other members of the community. Let them know how safe the school is and what progress has been made in making the school safer.
- Build partnerships with the business community and local law enforcement agencies.

Business and Community Leaders

- Adopt a local school by becoming more familiar with and addressing its needs in the context of the community. Develop an awareness of what works in reducing violence in the school, and build on past successes.
- Provide students with training in basic job skills, because the social skills commonly used in the work setting are similar to those required to prevent violence in the school setting.
- Provide students with employment opportunities—including internships, school-to-work programs, summer jobs, and after-school jobs— to help prevent and reduce criminal behavior.
- Provide scholarships and other incentives to deserving students.
- Sponsor extracurricular social and cultural activities and other positive activities for students.
- Offer resources to local schools, including programs, services, facilities for events, strategic planning, and equipment.
- Support working parents by providing them with flex-time scheduling opportunities. Encourage parents to attend parent-teacher conferences, field trips, meetings, mentoring sessions, and other school activities to strengthen their children's education.

Students

- Resolve problems and disputes nonviolently.
- Refrain from teasing, name-calling, and other forms of bullying.
- Respect all students, school staff, and family members.
- Know and follow school rules.
- Report crimes and threats of violence to school officials.
- Get involved in the development and implementation of anticrime programs at school.
- Learn how to avoid becoming a victim.
- Seek help from trusted adults when confronting difficult problems.

In Chapter 5, *Building a Leadership Culture,* ways will be explored for students, parents, business and community leaders, and educators to develop their leadership skills. This chapter will combine leadership and character development in a program for both adults and parents based on many of the strategies and model programs outlined in chapters Two and Four. For schools—educators, students, and parents (and community or business leaders), this program will be thought of as "never-ending." It will consist of continual training, dialogue, and skill enhancement involving character traits, problem-solving, adult-child discussion methods, and the development of conflict resolution skills.

School Violence, Risk, Preventive Intervention and Policy Illustrated Programs

In 1997, Daniel J. Flannery, Kent State University and the University Hospitals of Cleveland, provided a report on school violence, which outlined or illustrated several well-tested violence prevention programs. Flannery commented at the beginning of this report: "Sometimes teachers, administrators, parents, and others express a sense of hopelessness about the many challenges of youth violence and the role that schools play in promoting or reducing it. Historically there have been many attempts at quick fixes, an emphasis on maintaining social control rather than on improving school climate, and a dependence on approaches that have lacked any empirical data on effectiveness. Fortunately many schools have begun to shift their strategy. Part of the change results from necessity: these historical approaches have not worked very well and the problem of school violence is increasing. The need to garner additional resources has also increased as local communities struggle to support their schools and as school funding formulas are being reexamined (i.e., to establish greater equity between rich and poor districts). These resources will not come from the business community, foundations, or the Federal government without quality evaluation data for program effectiveness, even if the data are of a pilot nature and short term." We divide Flannery's report into program types, selection rationale, and illustrated programs.[5]

Program Types

Some programs focus on individual children identified by teachers or peers as aggressive or at risk for school failure. Decreasing individual risk of perpetrating violence at school then reduces school violence, or the potential for it. For example, if a program reduces a child's aggressive behavior and increases that child's problem-solving ability and social skills, the school will decrease the likelihood of the child instigating a fight with a peer or reacting with hostility to one of the many conflicts which occur at a school.

Other programs combine a focus on individual and family risk by integrating their school based programs with efforts to work with parents and families, peers, or community members. Still other programs integrate an individual risk focus with attempts to change the culture or environment of the school. These programs tend to place a lot of emphasis on the comportability of their strategies across people, settings, and places. The focus on changing the environment is meant to provide positive, long-term reinforcement to sustain individual behavior change.

Most programs have a dual focus: increasing student social skills and prosocial competence, and reducing aggressive behavior.

Selection Rationale

This section presents illustrative examples of some violence prevention programs that show promise as effective strategies. Three criteria generally guided the choice of examples.

1. Programs at the elementary, middle, and high school levels are described because they are generally very different in their focus, content, and purpose.
2. There is a focus on programs that are relatively well established. This is not to say that they are necessarily old, but that they have been adopted in many different locations. Even though few programs will work equally well in all settings and all geographic locations, there is also no need to reinvent wheels.
3. The sample includes programs that have undergone some level of evaluation of effectiveness. Intensive evaluation of school-based violence prevention programs is a relatively new phenomenon, for in the past more effort has been put into creating and implementing the programs than into evaluating them. By no means are these programs the only ones operating, and they are not necessarily the best models for

all schools and all situations. Indeed, other resources review additional school-based violence prevention programs. The programs discussed below should be viewed as specific, singular components of a comprehensive, long-term strategy to reduce school violence.

Illustrated Programs

The following are established programs that have been evaluated or are undergoing study for effectiveness. Most are geared for a particular age group, and some involve parents and the community.

ELEMENTARY SCHOOL PROGRAMS

Three elementary school–based programs are reviewed: Peace-Builders, which originated in Tucson, Arizona; Second Step, which originated in Seattle, Washington; and the Young Ladies/Young Gentlemen Clubs, from Cleveland, Ohio.

PeaceBuilders is a school-wide violence prevention program for students in grades K–5. It is currently operating in nearly 400 schools in Arizona, California, Utah, and Ohio. Implemented by both staff and students, the program incorporates a strategy to change the school climate. The purpose of this program is to develop and enhance prosocial behavior among children and staff, as well as a student's social competence, and to reduce aggressive behavior. The curriculum consists of five basic principles: (1) praise people, (2) avoid put-downs, (3) seek wise people as advisers and friends, (4) notice and correct the hurts you cause, and (5) right wrongs. Adults reinforce and model the behaviors at school, at home, and in public places. PeaceBuilders attempts to create a common language and culture that is easily transferable across people, settings, and time. The program provides extensive materials to teachers and parents, and incorporates community involvement and the media as resources to effect long-term systematic change.

PeaceBuilders is meant to become a "way of life" in both school and home. Some of the materials utilized by PeaceBuilders include praise notes for student positive behaviors and referrals to the principal's office for good behavior. Students identify with a Hero (themselves in comic books and activities) who resolves conflict and problem situations as a PeaceBuilder. Schools have a *wise person* lunch table where business and community leaders join PeaceBuilder—nominated students for a meal. Recently materials have been developed to utilize PeaceBuilder principles with at-risk and special needs children, as well as to address individual differences (e.g., culture and religion).

The program is currently in the middle of a 6-year longitudinal evaluation funded by the Centers for Disease Control and Prevention. The evaluation consists of both process and outcome data, including reports from students, teachers, and parents, and archival data from the schools and the local police department. Information on program implementation and utility is also being gathered, along with observations of playground behavior. The initial evaluation results from the program are very encouraging, reflecting teacher-rated increases in social competence and declines in aggressive behavior. Participating schools have also experienced reductions in student visits to the nurse's office for treatment of injuries compared to control schools.

The Second Step program also targets young children in grades 1-3, although it also has modules for students through grade 8. Second Step is designed to prevent aggressive behavior by increasing prosocial behavior, reflected by competence in peer interactions and in interpersonal conflict resolution skills. Based on the "habits of thought" model that violence can be unlearned, Second Step includes activities to help students acquire empathy, impulse control, problem solving, and anger management skills. A recent comprehensive and well-designed evaluation of the Second Step program showed that 2 weeks after the 30-lesson curriculum, students in the intervention group were rated by behavioral observers to be less physically aggressive and to engage in more neutral or positive behaviors on the playground and in the lunchroom (but not in the classroom) than students in the control group. Some of the changes persisted 6 months after the intervention, although neither teachers nor parents rated significant behavior change.

The third program is not as large or comprehensive as the other two, but illustrates an approach of early identification of at-risk youth. The Young Ladies/Young Gentlemen Clubs (YLYG) in the Cleveland Public Schools targets youth in grades 1-6 who are identified by teachers and principals as at risk for school failure and dropping out and who engage in problem behavior in the classroom. Students attend a group session several times per week directed by an adult who also serves as a mentor to the students and as a liaison between the student's family and the school (i.e., by conducting home visits). The group focuses on developing problem-solving and social skills, as well as on character education and discipline. Students learn how to respect and care for themselves, each other, and adults. Music therapy has proven to be a valuable factor in the program's success. YLYG, developed by the Partnership for a Safer Cleveland, has been in existence since the mid–1980s and has served as a model for similar programs in other school districts throughout the country.

YLYG has undergone several (albeit limited) evaluations. Analyses of grade card data found statistically significant improvements in positive classroom behaviors, self-control, and general attachment to school. Parents also reported program benefits: 96 percent said YLYG helped their child perform better at school, 92 percent that the club had helped their child's behavior at home, and 97 percent felt the YLYG is an important part of their child's education.

MIDDLE SCHOOL PROGRAMS

Conflict resolution is one of the most common approaches to violence prevention in middle schools and high schools. One of the most widely known is the *Resolving Conflicts Creatively Program* (RCCP) in New York City. It has models for implementation for children in grades K–12 and is a comprehensive school-based program in conflict resolution and intercultural understanding. Its curricula contain strategies to promote multicultural acceptance and global peace. Teachers are trained first, then student mediators are taught to address conflict with nonviolent alternatives and negotiation skills. Mediators work in pairs during lunch periods and recess to identify and resolve disputes.

Conflict resolution programs, while extremely popular and widespread, have not generally fared well in the face of intensive evaluation. While several intensive longitudinal evaluations of RCCP are ongoing and the final verdict is yet to come, early research on conflict mediation programs has shown few long-term effects in reducing violent behavior or risk of victimization. One potential problem faced by conflict mediation programs was identified above: they tend to focus on mediating only the most serious conflicts, which differentially reinforces them when they occur.

Other examples of promising middle school-based programs include the **Students for Peace Project** and the **Richmond Youth Against Violence Project.** Students for Peace seeks to modify the school environment, promote peer leadership, and educate parents and students about violence prevention. The Richmond Project focuses on African American middle school students in an urban setting. Its 16-session program, Responding in Peaceful and Positive Ways, promotes positive and healthy alternatives to interpersonal and situational violence. Both these programs are currently undergoing intensive longitudinal evaluations.

High School Programs

While many high school students are exposed to conflict mediation programs, several other kinds of interventions are more prevalent with older students. These include job training, mentoring, and rites of passage programs. Violence prevention at the high school level also focuses more frequently on delinquent youth and those at risk for gang involvement, such as the **Omega Boys Club** in San Francisco, California.

Self-Enhancement, Inc., in Portland, Oregon, is a grassroots, community-service organization that provides services to at-risk middle and high school youth. The program works primarily at the individual and interpersonal level to build resilience and promote the pursuit of healthy, productive lives. The program consists of classroom activities, exposure education, and proactive education. Classroom education focuses on anger management, conflict resolution, and problem solving. Exposure education consists of field trips to community agencies. Proactive education involves students in assemblies, media productions, and newsletters, which are created to promote nonviolence.

Parent/Community/School Partnerships

One of the most consistent findings from school-based violence prevention programs is that parent involvement is extremely important to the success and maintenance of any intervention. Programs with a home and school focus typically include parent workshops or training sessions on such topics as monitoring, effective discipline, increasing parent involvement at school, effectively modeling a positive attachment to school, and endorsing positive values related to educational achievement. Partnerships also stress increased parent awareness and buy-in of school expectations and consequences for failure to complete schoolwork or for discipline problems. The most effective school programs are the ones that have parent support, with parents backing up school limits and consequences at home. Such support also facilitates communication between school staff and parents about children who are experiencing difficulties. It is extremely important that interventions be introduced early, as soon as indicators for significant behavior problems first emerge.

Clearinghouse on Urban Education "Safe School Model"

The Clearinghouse on Urban Education has provided a public-private partnership model for school safety called the "Safe School Model."[6] In the introduction to this model, the Clearinghouse states, "To provide a safe educational environment and a safe haven for our next generations, teachers, parents, and students must work together. It is understood that without a steadfast approach and response from all stakeholders, it will not just happen. It is our responsibility to do something to stop social deterioration. To overcome the unsafe school environment we are proposing a safe school model. This will be achieved through a public-private partnership. The Public-Private Partnership Model stems from the belief that anything can be achieved if everyone actively participates in the process and puts their best efforts forward.

"We all recognize that the school environment is not as safe as it should be. By simply recognizing this fact only, we cannot make any difference. Should we like to make a positive change in decaying school environments, we all must believe in this fact, we all must live with this fact, and combine our efforts for a positive change. When the majority of our stakeholders think that there is a need for a change and everyone works towards that change, then change will occur.

"Since we believe that a change is needed in the public school environment, we must act together. Our public private partnership model will include school administrations, school staff, parents, guardians, students, neighborhood organizations, and law enforcement agencies. In teamwork, these issues can be discussed in an open forum and policies will be generated based on consensus. To formulate acceptable policies there should be some ground rules, which are based on trust and mutual respect." The model proposed by the Clearinghouse on Urban Education is composed of the following steps:

Establish Trust and Respect. The most important task for the whole group is trust. Trust must prevail throughout the program, among teachers and staff, and between all participants. Without trust nothing can be achieved. All the problems we are encountering in the school system are due to lack of trust between students, between students and teachers, and between parents and teachers.

Another important issue is respect. In this society, respect has deteriorated to an alarming level. Morale of a society diminishes with the decrease of mutual respect and mutual trust among fellow citizens. A main goal of this program is to achieve a healthy society, where children will learn and grow in a peaceful environment. Everybody agrees that childhood should be a protected and blooming time in the human life cycle. Social morale cannot be improved without improving the trust and respect among the participants within society.

Develop Communication Between Parents and Guardians. The importance of parent involvement in resolving these problems is significant. As in the case of the Columbine High School shootings, the parents of victim Brooks Brown knew of threats made before the massacre by Eric Harris, one of the assailants. The Brown family was afraid for the life of their son. Eric's website noted that he would like to kill lot of people, including Brooks Brown. The Brown family informed the police, who took no action. Harris was so violent that the Brown family was afraid to bring the issue to his father. Although Mrs. Brown and Mrs. Klebold (mother of assailant Dylan Klebold) were friends for years, still Mrs. Brown did not consider informing her about the content of her son's friend Eric's website. Mrs. Brown even did not allow Mr. Brown to call or fax a printout of the page to Mr. Harris, thinking that it might only provoke Eric to violence. Recalling their previous experience, Mrs. Brown was sure that Mr. Harris would not discipline his son.

There was a time when parents used to talk to each other and resolve issues, but nowadays we can see that they do not communicate with each other. As a result, we witness tragedy. Communications play an important role in children's behavior. If our children are not well behaved, we must devise a method so that their behavior can be changed. The issue is how well we communicate with our children. A proactive communication, identifying the problems they are facing, can resolve many problems and keep them from becoming deeply rooted in a child's mind. The violence at Columbine demonstrates that parents failed to provide adequate communications for their children's problems. Should they have done so, the story would have been different.

Observe Children Attentively. It is practically impossible to assume that the assailants' parents had not observed anything unusual in their children's behavior. Some argue that they must have observed something unusual in their children's behavior, but they did not act accordingly or failed to discipline these boys. The *Time* magazine December 20, 1999, issue noted that one of the Columbine students, Nathan Dykeman (although a problematic witness) reported that Eric told him that Eric's father found a pipe bomb at their house, which Eric and his father took out and detonated. On one occasion the Brown family complained to Mr. Harris regarding the throwing of an ice ball at their car, but Mr. Harris did not discipline his son. On another occasion, the clerk of a weapons store called Harris' house and said, "Hey your clips are in." Mr. Harris received the phone call and responded that he did not order any clips. The clerk had mistakenly informed Eric's father, thinking that he was talking to Eric. Mr. Harris did not even inquire as to whether the clerk was dialing the right number. Based on the published information, it appears that Mr. Harris took no appropriate action, especially in the case of gun clips, knowing that Eric had a bad reputation and that Eric and Dylan Klebold had served one year of community service for a past crime.

Seek Help from Professionals. When our children are out of control, we should seek help from other sources. Help can come from the parents of our children's friends, school administrations, or from law enforcement agencies. In this high-risk society we must act appropriately. If we take the information in the previous paragraph as true, we can come to two possible conclusions: Eric's parents communicated with Eric and tried to change his way of life, which did not work, or the parents did not take any action. Perhaps the outcome would have been different if the parents of the assailants had sought outside intervention. These boys were sick; they needed adequate treatment. They were frustrated and emotionally vulnerable. Most of the students at the school knew that; most of the neighbors might have noticed that. To be sick is not a crime. It was our failure to take appropriate measures, to provide them with adequate treatment.

Speak Up and Bring Problems Out into the Open. One of the easiest ways we can get rid of any kind of frustration is to bring things out in the open. This can done by discussing the problem with others, i.e., sharing. Although dialogue is not a miracle cure, it can expose problems and allow children to vent their emotions and frustrations. When we speak to others about any problem, it releases some of our pain, thereby reducing or eliminating the frustration. Also, those we share our frustrations with may help to resolve the problem. Therefore, it is important to share our pains with others.

Actively Listen to Children. Children feel comfortable when they feel important. In the absence of internalized importance, they feel abandoned. In a good society children are less greedy than elders. They do not lie, they do not harm others, and they like to live a stress-free life. They do not believe in differences, they think that all are equal.

Children today are intelligent, but in some cases they are diverting their intelligence in the wrong direction. Of course, children fight each other one day and the next day they are friends again. Their animosities are not deep-rooted. As they are the most vulnerable class of the society because it is easy to manipulate them. It is easy to use them in a wrong way. We need to set boundaries for our children so that the negative impact of their society cannot penetrate their emotional environment. It is surely not an easy task, but should we all try, we can make a difference.

Adults Need to Be Open and Trustworthy. Children spend more of their time in the school than they spend at their home. Hence, the school environment can have a huge impact on their behavior. To improve children's behavior, we first must attempt to fix the problem in the school environment (what educators refer to as the "school climate"). The school environment is the environment of social interaction between children, teachers, administrative staff, bus drivers, security personnel, and others who spend some time every day at the school. If we make it a healthy environment for our children, positive behavior can be achieved immediately.

Many incidents at school demonstrate the lack of trust between students and school officials. At Columbine, some children reported, after the incident, that they had been very much scared of the gang that included Harris and Klebold. No one spoke up because they thought that they would be in trouble should these "guys" know about any complaints. It is clear from this news that there was a lack of communication between children and school administration at Columbine. It demonstrates that there was a lack of trust between children and teachers. Could the children trust their teachers, they should have brought the issue to them, and the problem could have been handled differently. Then the whole story would have been different. We missed that opportunity due to lack of trust.

Hold the School Responsible. There is a trend that the school administration does not report to outside authorities any suspicious activities in their school. They have a fear that if they report about these, it will create a public outcry and as a result the school will lose students, and therefore funding based on enrollment. The federal, state, and local governments need to restructure their budgets; the focus should be not on numbers but on quality and safe environments. There is much information today on how to create a safe school environment. Administrators need to create a checklist of important variables and improve all areas that are weak and ineffective.

Establish Academic Achievement as a Core Program for All Students. Social problems always spill over into the school system, since teachers, staffs, and children are all part of the society. It is very hard to isolate the school from social problems. No matter how hard we try, or how much money we spend, we will still see the effects of social problems in the school environment. However, we can create in each school a *basic academic environment*, which means an environment where children will learn how to become respectable citizens. We are talking about the learning process through sharing, and allowing all children and school staff and teachers to focus on quality improvement and target their sole mission toward excelling life. This is an environment in which everyone will forget about their background, race, and culture, and will believe and act to demonstrate that being different is beneficial. Academic achievement should be a priority for all school districts.

Establish Effective Communications Between the School, Law Enforcement and Other Agencies. It is important to establish a good communication system among the schools and other agencies. Schools should have proactive evacuation plans to handle emergency situations. According to the *Time* magazine December 20, 1999, issue, nearly 800 police officers and SWAT team members were present at the school compound soon after the news of school shooting at Columbine broke out. The whole team was in chaos; they were not properly equipped nor did they have the building plans. Eric and Dylan were carrying out their shooting for more than 45 minutes, but police could not identify their location. If a good communications system between the school and the law enforcement agencies had been in place, it would have been possible to save several lives. Both the killers were dead by 12:05 p.m., but the SWAT team did not reach Sanders (the dead teacher at Columbine) until close to 3:00 p.m.

We must be better prepared. We must have emergency evacuation plans and a decent communications system in place. Schools should be equipped with appropriate surveillance systems, so that authorities can get accurate pictures of inside school buildings from a remote location. We do not want to see a repetition of Columbine, where law enforcement agents were standing by helplessly and asking distraught children to draw the layout of the sprawling of the 250,000 square foot school building.

CONCLUSION

The Clearing House on Urban Education concluded that several societal changes are necessary to establish safe schools. The Clearing House summarized: "These changes must take the form of changed values, good communications, increased understanding between parents and children and among children. Information is needed to allow all concerned to effect change. The kind of information necessary can best be made available on an interactive website for everyone to access and to provide responses. Knowledge that is received in advance will help in deterring crime and will contribute mightily to solutions sorely needed for our schools in coping with safety issues."

5

Building a
Leadership Culture

The major components and strategies for creating a school safety and antiviolence program have been carefully outlined in both Chapters 3 and 4. In Chapter 4, some of the highest-rated programs in the nation where mentioned, programs that have been professionally evaluated and show promise in preventing school violence or altering the antisocial and violent behaviors of students. As was mentioned, the very best of these programs include all the major players in the school profile: students and their parents, community leaders, teachers, and school administrators.

Support for school safety initiatives comes from three major sources: the federal government, state governments, and private resource centers, associations, and alliances. In Chapter 2, the major initiatives of both the federal government and state governments were mentioned. Chapter 6 is an alphabetical listing of national resource centers, associations, and alliances. Many of these are private, but some are government sponsored.

Because this is a resource book, no effort has been made to develop a definitive school safety program. This book's major purpose has been to alert you to the best possible resources available on school safety strategies and programs. However, there is a perceived need to provide you with more detailed information about several of the key strategies mentioned in Chapters 3 and 4. For instance, character education has been discussed as a component in many of the initiatives in school safety; therefore the major components of a character education program need to be outlined. At the same time, training students and parents in conflict resolution, creative problem solving, and decision-making are also recommended as key elements of school safety programs, especially those with long-range consequences. It does seem appropriate to put these strategies together contextually to demonstrate how they might work in a school safety program. Providing additional information about these strategies will assist educational professionals in building their own long-term school safety initiatives around such long-term courses of action as training, counseling, and home-school applications.

An additional area that appears to be neglected in this discussion is "leadership." Although many books have been written about "leadership," and training guides of all sorts have been developed, the majority of this material is aimed at the business community. Only recently have leadership training programs been developed for students and educators. In the future, we hope to see more of this material adapted for educators, parents, and students. To prevent violence in schools and communities, parents, students, and educators must "lead the way" by modeling anti-violent and positive social behaviors. By definition, leaders have a clear vision and a set of operating principles for their work and they live what they think and believe. A leader is someone others are willing to follow. Of course, there are students and adults who lead in negative and unethical ways. To prevent this kind of leadership from developing in schools, we must build a leadership culture that is based on ethical principles. The essence of this kind of leadership is the desire to serve one another and to serve something beyond us. Joining leadership with the components of a strong character education program will, in this way, allow us to build anti-violent and school safety programs that are easily assimilated into the curriculum of the school without the burden of a lot of add-ons and extra work for teachers and staff.

Leadership: A Calculus of Potential

Character educators have correctly emphasized building ethical leadership skills among students.[1] This is an important part of the task and mission of our schools. But as we think about building a leadership culture in our schools, the applications of this concept cannot be

limited to students. Rather, the challenge is for all school professionals, especially teachers, to become leaders in their classrooms, in their
schools, and among their peers. Also, any program that focuses on
school safety issues, leadership, problem solving, or conflict resolution
must be inclusive. The emphasis is on changing behaviors—the behaviors of students, teachers, parents, administrators, and other school
personnel. No one can be excluded for such a program to work. We
learned this in Chapters 3 and 4. Therefore, we add participatory leadership to one of the needs of a school safety program.

Participatory Leadership

Participatory leadership has become the ideal, not only in schools,
but in business and the community as well. Participatory leadership,
according to Phillip Schlechty,[2] will focus on teachers and students as
knowledge-workers. He believes that schools need to be re-invented
with this idea in mind. He says that as schools become more knowl-
edge-based and school work becomes more knowledge work, students
will be viewed as knowledge workers and not as products to be herded,
tested, and branded (maintained). Likewise, teachers will become
guides to information resources rather than providers of information.
Teachers will begin teaching students how to learn and will develop
them as thinkers, problem-solvers, and conflict-resolvers—as creators
of their own information.

It was Peter Drucker[3] who reminded us that we live in a world
where change is the rule rather than the exception. What is required
in this kind of world is a *calculus of potential* rather than one of statistical probability. Drucker does not suggest that we throw out accountability and all that it implies, but that we should understand much
more is involved in human learning and productivity, in the education of a child, and the changing of lifestyles than standardized methods, curricula, and evaluations. Building a school safety program from
the point of view of a calculus of potential will involve the creativity,
insights, and innovations of all key personnel involved, including students and their parents.

This is quickly becoming the new environment of learning in our
schools. Can we become leaders in this new environment? Can students be treated with respect and will they treat others with respect

and dignity in this new age? We cannot forget to examine our values, for effective leadership is driven by one's character, which includes our motivation to lead, our beliefs and values and our purpose as educators. It is our purpose, beliefs, and values, which shape our vision and day-to-day activities. As we work with youngsters and their parents to create anti-violence and school safety programs, it will be our integrity, commitment, truthfulness, and honesty that create the foundation for success. These values, if we model them consistently, embrace our goals, and when aligned with our behaviors and school-based practices, will determine our success.

Today, schools find themselves in an exciting, albeit frustrating, paradigm shift, where new methods and new programs are trying to capture the value-shift that began in the 1960s. The 19th century workplace model developed by Frederick Taylor in 1881—for the purpose of standardizing and controlling industrial production and adopted by schools for sorting and selecting students for placement in college or the industrial complex—has been replaced in business and industry, while schools continue use this model with its standardized curricula, testing, and teacher-performance criteria.[4]

We should remember that prior to 1960, the purpose of transportation was to move people; after that time, it has been to move information. Today, participatory leadership is based on the quality of the educational culture and the respect that moves both ways through the system from top to bottom and from bottom to top. Participatory leadership is managing by values:

- Students and their parents, teachers and administrators are all valued as human beings and as important to the educational process.
- Participatory leadership, which moves by trust, creates an innovative environment that values the contribution of all who are involved in it.
- A trusting environment is a growth environment in which resources are directed toward opportunities for improvement in both teaching and learning.
- An environment of trust makes and maintains connections important to the life of the organization, and it is accountable.

The Teacher as Servant-Leader

Current leadership research provides a significant checklist of skills and behaviors needed for becoming effective, efficient leaders. We begin with the term "servant-leader," first coined by Robert K. Greenleaf in 1970.[5] The concept of "servant-leader" is further developed by Kevin Cashman,[6] who says that to become effective leaders, we must:

- Live what we think and believe.
- Establish a clear vision and a set of operating beliefs and values.
- Develop a mission and live by it.
- Find consensus in the organization about core values among those with whom we work.
- Align day-to-day practices with our values.
- Follow the best interests of those whom we lead.
- Gain satisfaction from the growth of others.
- Be accountable for our behavior and the behavior of those who follow us.
- Be willing to listen.
- Give obedience to a higher mission than serving our own egos.
- Manage by our values.
- Live with integrity and lead by example.
- Develop a winning strategy that focuses on student success and self-development.
- Manage change, set priorities, create a vision, and be trustworthy.
- Invite others to share our authority and knowledge, and the responsibility for student success.
- Inspire our peers to achieve success.
- Focus on innovation. Respond to a variety of different needs.
- Let student success drive our teaching.
- Become results-oriented by empowering students with knowledge about how to learn.
- Get students actively engaged in working on and with knowledge.
- Encourage intelligent risk-taking among students.
- Make decisions that solve, rather than create, problems.

Building any program in the school requires individuals who will step up to the plate and offer their services. The concepts of participatory leadership and servant leadership require those initiating school safety and anti-violence programs to check their egos at the door. Teachers and administrators need to remember that they are made great by the accomplishments of their peers and their students. Any school safety program needs to integrate the best principles of management and leadership, of innovation and stability, and order and flexibility into building a true leadership culture. It was Peter Drucker who said, "If we do things the way they have always been done, we will get what we have always gotten."[7]

Character Education

The concept of "leadership" outlined above blends naturally with the precepts of character education. Patient leadership is required to effectively educate children in ethical values and the foundations of civility. Patience generates the opportunity for understanding and understanding begs for open dialogue—for conversation—where there is give-and-take of ideas, of problems, and solutions. Here is where children discover meaning and begin to grow intuitively and spiritually. Self-esteem and personal meaning are those inner qualities that affirm the significance of our lives.[8]

A child builds moral character by continuously having his or her life affirmed through love and praise. A positive relationship with parents, teachers, and peers gives meaning to the child's life. Research cited in Chapters 3 and 4, has demonstrated the relationship between developing positive self-esteem, purpose and direction in life, and positive social or civil behaviors. Perhaps one of the greatest gifts we are able to give children is empowering them with the knowledge and will to make ethical decisions. When their vision of the future is blurred— or doesn't exist except in some limited and negative ways—their motivation for living ethically with others is also diminished. Cliff Havener says that under these circumstances, they end up doing nonsensical things.[9]

To educate children in ethical behaviors is to provide opportunities for them to enrich their lives. These will include times when they can provide services to others and when they can provide leadership for activities that enrich the lives of others. To imprint their lives with moral standards and to rationally adjust these as their experiences dictate is a task of not only teaching and discipline, but of modeling these behaviors ourselves. Our faithfulness to this commitment must be seriously addressed, for anything that falls short of this goal will not have a positive impact on the developing civility of our students and children.

So long as conversations between adults (teachers, parents, ministers, etc.) and children continue; so long as we allow children to be children and do not treat them as miniature adults; so long as we teach them to care and respect all living things, including themselves; and so long as an ethical foundation for character development is built within the family unit, continued in the school, and gradually extended to a wider community of persons with a sense of social justice and commitment, there is hope for a better tomorrow.

Character education is necessary in our schools and should become a solid part of every school safety program. It is preventive, but even for those children and students designated as violent or recognized as having a strong propensity for violence, character education can have an educational effect. Effective character education programs demonstrate a different way of life and sustains open discussion of problems, but are completely honest about answers and the hard work it takes to turn one's life around. When educators commit themselves to both the academic and moral growth of children, they are committing themselves to the creation of a moral future.

In June 1989, the Carnegie Council on Adolescent Development[10] prepared a report focusing attention on the needs of youth for the 21st century. The report said to help children acquire durable self-esteem, develop flexible and inquiring habits of mind, and nurture reliable and close human relationships, we have to emphasize the importance of their belonging to a valued group where they attain a sense of usefulness in themselves. The Council outlined the following five characteristics which they associated with becoming productive citizens in the 21st century:

1. Becoming intellectually reflective,
2. Being en route to a lifetime of meaningful work,

3. Becoming good citizens,
4. Developing caring and ethical habits,
5. Staying physically and mentally healthy.

The ethical values emphasized by the Council included courage, acceptance of responsibility, honesty, integrity, tolerance, appreciation of individual differences, and caring about others. The report envisioned that our children will have developed the capacity of thinking accurately and clearly, and will have developed the ability to behave ethically. In 1987, the second edition of the *Philosophy for Young Thinkers* (PYT) curriculum stated, "The vacuum caused by a generation of uncertainty about teaching values and the move away from a traditional values-base at home is just now having its impact on our schools. Our answer to this social and educational dilemma is the production of a morally centered, pre-college philosophy curriculum for our students. In this curriculum we shall argue for and provide a foundation for teaching such moral values as honesty, integrity, responsibility, honor, courage, and kindness."[11] The PYT curriculum pointed out the growing need for developing the following behaviors:

- Flexible attitudes and abilities that will help students when confronted with difficult educational and social challenges,
- The discovery of better and more creative solutions to urgent problems,
- The retention of intellectual and emotional flexibility, and
- The maintenance of a universal and unbiased vision of people and their role in one's future.

Components

In the book *Jefferson's Children,* Leon Botstein says, "Without an environment of hope and optimism, nothing we do in the school and for the school will help. The reason for this rests in the influence that hopelessness has on our sense of time. It shortens our vision."[12] School safety and character education programs should have as a major part of their mission to show children the future and give them hope that they can help make things better. We must remember that "character" is our most inner talent exercised with courage. The schools can become a common mooring for our children's moral development, supporting their desire to exercise their moral courage. With families and other government agencies, they can become a working union of the ideal and the actual that take into account the limits and dependency of human life.

There are six fundamental components of a solid character education program. These are: developing a supportive home and classroom environment; examining value choices through listening and dialogue; talking with children about making ethical choices; helping children develop problem-solving skills; building relationships and resolving conflicts; and building character through service.

DEVELOPING A SUPPORTIVE HOME AND CLASSROOM ENVIRONMENT

Aaron Lynch says that an essential factor in the process of teaching children the virtue of living by ethical principles is the degree to which children feel loved by their parents.[13] Children who feel loved can more easily believe that their parents spread ideas to them for their own good. Children who persistently feel unloved by their parents, however, may conclude that the parents dictate values mainly for their own self-interests rather than their, the children's, interest. Lynch points out that, in reality, some children do not follow their parents' teaching about ethical behavior. On the other hand, he says that children whose parents are actively involved in living by ethical principles will normally live by these principles themselves. Love for children is contagious and can enhance the development of a child's ethical values in simple and direct ways.

Children are enriched through interactions with their parents, teachers, and other significant adults. Likewise, when our children respond to our teaching in positive, ethical ways, they enrich our lives in a manner that is often unexplainable, but brings us great joy. Within the family and the school, a child's character is continuously refined through this process of dialogue, modeling, and direct teaching. Growth is interactive—the moral dispositions that define character begin early in the home and are cultivated through a natural interplay of the child with his or her playmates, extended family, peers, and teachers.

There are several "getting started" activities for parents and teachers to strengthen their character education initiative.

Clarify your beliefs about children. As you do this, remember that beliefs form a way of life, a philosophy of life; they develop over time and will change with time; they are not hard and fast rules; and from them we can formulate goals and objectives for educating our children and students.

Consider the following:

- Children can live harmoniously through combining personal satisfactions and self-development with significant work that contributes to the welfare of the family, school, and community.
- Children will develop faith in others if adults have faith in them.
- Children can tap their own powers to solve difficult problems if adults teach them to reason and share their responses.
- A child's uniqueness will unfold quite naturally as adults express respect for his or her abilities as well as possibilities.
- Each child possesses intrinsic moral and intellectual work and we should look upon them, as well as ourselves, as both natural and good.
- Children do not have to grow at the expense of others.
- Children are naturally open and responsive to their environment; therefore, we must involve them in discussions of values, model positive, growth-producing behaviors for them, and encourage their own immersion in our institutions and traditions.
- Finally, children are naturally creative and the more they learn and practice intellectually and ethically, the more abundantly they will produce for themselves and for their families and communities.

Evaluate the real time that is spent with children discussing character issues and helping them resolve their problems and clarify concerns. James Q. Wilson said, "A moral life is perfected by practice more than by precept; children are not taught so much as habituated. In this sense the schools inevitably teach morality, whether they intend to or not, by such behavior as they reward or punish. A school reinforces the better moral nature of a pupil to the extent it insists on the habitual performance of duties, including the duty to deal fairly with others, to discharge one's own responsibilities, and to defer the satisfaction of immediate and base motives in favor of more distant and nobler ones."[14]

What is needed is for both parents to evaluate the quality time they spend with their children each day and week. Teachers, too, need to evaluate the time they spend each week discussing issues of character and civility with children. Once we have made our evaluations, then careful planning needs to occur so that we will have time to impact our children's developing moral dispositions and problem solving abilities. At school, if there is a character education curriculum or initiative, don't waste it on trivial matters. Plan, be committed to, and use this time positively with your students.

Developing a supportive home and classroom environment means helping children build an ethical foundation for the present and the future. Six steps or building blocks will aid parents and teachers with the task:

- Collaborative thinking is thinking together; it is "we-ness" thinking. Collaborative thinking will widen our vision and help children create the capacity for love and empathy on a larger scale. It helps them learn to take other people's needs into consideration when making decisions, develop the capacity for fair-mindedness, and understand the concept and application of equality.
- Commitment to mastery is important for academic and future success. This doesn't mean dominance. Rather, it means proficiency. As children grow they should be given the opportunity to master certain skills, clarify and deepen their commitments and focus their energies on things they love to do.
- We need to help children cleanse the windows from which they view the larger world. These windows are frames of reference that provide direction and the motivation to achieve. As we enlarge and cleanse our windows, we also discover we have the ability to acknowledge with care the variations and differences in others and ourselves.

- Sharing a positive vision of the future is also important for redirecting violent or anti-social behaviors. Teachers and parents who sustain a measure of influence and stability in their classrooms and homes share common missions, goals, and beliefs that are deeply valued. When teachers and parents model ethical behaviors, and live them authentically, they are able to share with their children and students their inspired vision of the future and their beliefs and values.

- Learning together is important to building character and trust in children. Shared learning begins in nonjudgmental dialogue and results in a genuine pattern of "thinking together." Our children learn to accept the world as it is, and may be motivated to make positive changes in their own communities by sensing they have an important role to play within it.

- The final building block is self-control. Building an ethical society requires self-control, which means consistency of behavior and the ability to handle problems efficiently and effectively. When we model self-control, our children and students are more apt to practice it as well.

Ideas for improving the home and classroom environment can be summed up in the following eight steps:

1. Make sure there is an open sharing of important information, ideas and opinions.

2. Help children learn important concepts and skills related to social and group interactions.

3. Encourage children and students to express and share their feelings and emotions.

4. Allow children and students to maintain their individuality and personal integrity.

5. Deal with conflict and stress openly and quickly, searching for honest alternatives and creative solutions with which family members, students and teachers can live.

6. Utilize cooperative activities as a way of breaking down barriers to communication.

7. Emphasize children's successes as positive reinforcers for building self-esteem.

8. Avoid being judgmental, controlling all that the child or student says and does, manipulating children by using strategizing behaviors, neutral behaviors that do not demonstrate feelings and empathy toward children, and know-it-all behaviors that have no purpose except to demonstrate superiority.

EXAMINING VALUE CHOICES THROUGH LISTENING AND DIALOGUE

Children need to learn about value choices. Our role as parents and teachers is to inspire dramatic conversations about behaviors, events, and ideas that are significant to their learning and growth. When we talk and listen, we can see ourselves in others as they share the same needs and goals that we also have. The hope of creating an ethical community remains alive so long as these conversations continue. Our motivation to talk with our children about ideas and values should be to understand and guide, not to produce uniformity. Open conversation and tentative explanations will build a network of possibilities for our children. Listening is most important, for when we listen to our children, we will begin to hear the tone and recognize the pattern of their ethical choices.

What we learn from dialogue is that we can grow with our children. If we send them off to participate in separate activities, we cease to grow with them. In fact, we begin to get dormant. Dialogue with children provides an exceptional opportunity for them to teach us and for them to learn from us. Knowledge, like wisdom, flows both ways and comes through human interaction. Through dialogue we begin to transform ourselves and learn that we cannot come to know the qualities in our children without being able to bring those qualities to birth within ourselves.

One way to acknowledge the growth of children and students is to record their ideas. We need to take time to listen to what children have to say. We also need to mark the growth of their understanding and perhaps some of the exact words they use to explain their world. To help children grow in character, be prepared to discuss the following concepts with them, making sure to give examples of behaviors that illustrate each concept. Don't rush these conversations. Let them unfold quite naturally. The concepts are the following:

Respect. Our attachment and responsibility to our children must rest on a foundation of love and respect. A response to children based on whim and emotion is both inconsistent and fleeting. Consider the following: Respect is acknowledging and living a life that thinks of others as an extension of oneself. Respect asks the question: "What can I give to others that might improve their lives?" When lives are improved, all life will become better.

Trust. Each person has a desire to be trusted. Children are no exception. The social importance of honesty, truthfulness, and fair-mindedness brings out the meaning of "trust." Consider: Trust is the foundation of family and community. It is the guiding principle of a democratic nation. It is the behavior that builds friendship and is the cornerstone of self-discipline.

Honesty. Honesty is a mark of a virtuous person. Living a life committed to honesty is living a life that is morally stable. We must encourage our children to think about their behavior. With honesty, constructive criticism, and motivation we can help them create a moral, ethical society. We can positively affect our schools and communities when our family values are saturated with desirable ethical traits.

Friendship. One of the most positive ways of building character in children is stressing the importance and qualities of friendship. Consider: There is nothing automatic about friendship; it is built over time and is built on a foundation of honesty, trust, love, equality, respect, and fair play.

Responsibility. Responsibility means that we develop our lives with the intention of not just modifying our behavior for the sake of others, but that we help preserve the integrity and dignity of all of life. Responsibility awakens us to the realization that we are, in effect, trustees of a wonderful human heritage; that children are not our possession—they are our future and the future of humanity.

Consistency. Although not a moral term, "consistency" affects how we live. For example, consistency of character means "reliability" and "stability." It implies honesty and trustworthiness. The absence of consistency will mean that our behavior will be so erratic that others will not know what to expect from us or when to expect it. Ethical consistency is important in parenting, teaching, and in modeling positive civil behaviors for our children. Without consistency, our children will not develop ethical behaviors that are reliable and trustworthy.

Commitment. We can encourage love and diminish hate by committing ourselves to behave ethically toward others and do our best to practice civil and moral values in our lives. Our inconsistency in living ethically and our lack of commitment to ethical and moral principles diminish our ethical influence over others, especially our children.

Fair-Mindedness. Fair-mindedness means that we live our lives as people of good will; that we work fruitfully for the betterment of the lives of our families, students, and fellow humans. The simplicity of being fair-minded should not be underestimated. Children are taught by example both the habits and rewards of just behavior. Being fair-minded reveals a generosity of spirit and our willingness to treat others impartiality. Teaching children to be fair-minded allows them to put themselves in the place of others, to adopt their "position in life," so that they are able to see and feel as others see and feel.

TALKING WITH CHILDREN
ABOUT MAKING ETHICAL CHOICES

Talking with children and students about problems and situations they might find themselves in helps them gain perspective. Conversation helps our children mature intellectually, socially, and emotionally. Through conversation (dialogue) we are able to enrich their "inner wealth" that will enable them to live morally coherent lives.

A significant part of a sound character education program is talking with children about behaviors that matter. Open and sustained dialogue about topics which adults and children bring to the table is an important sign of our respect and care for them. Shutting children out of our lives by refusing to talk with them about problems and listen to their questions sends a message that we do not care for them or respect their ideas. Parents who care enough to take time to listen and understand, console, and support their children build families. Likewise, teachers who are caring and sensitive create effective learning environments. An effective character education and school safety program is built on this foundation.

The following are some guidelines for enriching child's understanding of ethical dilemmas.

1. Aligning family, school, classroom, and religious values is important for consistency when discussing moral dilemmas and conflicting situations with children.

2. Set aside time for group decision-making. Have discussions in which values are clarified and evaluated.

3. Identify those values that are vital and make a list. Keep them posted in easy view.

4. With your children or with your students, create a vision statement, which outlines your purposes and is consistent with your ethical values. Keep it posted and in easy view. Review this statement whenever necessary as a guide to the behavior of your classroom and family.

5. With your children and students, brainstorm ways to follow this vision statement at school, home, and during recreational activities.

6. Remember: respect is a value we all wish others would bestow on us. It is also a value we must be willing to give others. Our children's characters depend, to a large degree, on the level of respect we have for them. Respect lifts barriers between persons while a common vision and purpose unite the group.

Some guidelines for effective communication include the following:

1. Responsibility is taken by each person for his or her own behaviors and feelings. Don't expect others to read your mind.

2. Communicate directly with the person who is having a problem. Do not work through others. Children perceive greater strength of purpose in adults when adults work together and act together.

3. Don't speak critically about others behind their back unless you are willing to voice your criticism to their face.

4. State your views before asking how others feel about them. Don't set children up to give a wrong answer and then put them down for saying it.

5. Practice active listening. This is one way of building and maintaining communication and respect.

6. Provide continual feedback and keep open all lines of communication between yourself and the young people in your care or your own children. Don't allow resentments to build and do not forget to give positive feedback.

7. Respect and validate the youngster's feelings. Congratulate them on small achievements and they will more than likely listen to you when the stakes are higher. Remember that communication is to relationships what breathing is to maintaining life.

HELPING CHILDREN DEVELOP PROBLEM-SOLVING SKILLS

Problem solving is a necessary tool for both ethical and academic growth. It is highly recommended in all the school safety programs mentioned in Chapters 3 and 4. We have learned in research on critical thinking that problem solving is an activity which engages and stimulates the learner in the movement toward problem or conflict resolution.[15] When children learn to reason, they will be better prepared to generate new ideas, make more sound decisions, and resolve difficult personal or social problems.

In any school, thinking and reasoning should be the foundation of curricula, teaching, and character development. Teaching for thinking—problem solving—is not just another add-on program, but a means of accomplishing all of the school's objectives, sustaining creative and productive lives, and helping children become productive citizens. This is why it is imperative for parents to provide guidance for their children in problem solving and decision-making. It is also important that teachers and parents are trained in the rudiments of problem solving and decision making themselves. This begins with instruction and practice in applying critical thinking to academic concerns and then moves forward to more personal and social areas.

Teaching children to become more efficient problem solvers and decision makers begins in the home and should continue throughout their years in school. With this mission in mind, the following five goals should permeate any program in character education and school safety:

1. To provide a learning environment adapted to the needs of children, which concentrates on such areas as creative and critical thinking, mathematical adeptness, the mastery of content, and the ability to communicate in writing and speaking.
2. To provide opportunities for students to enhance, develop, and utilize their originality, initiatives, and self-motivation.

3. To assist students with the development of affective (ethical, moral, spiritual and emotional) and valuing skills.

4. To provide educational activities which incorporate multimedia and multidisciplinary approaches to learning.

5. To help students take responsibility for setting personal goals, provide an environment in which students can develop productive peer relationships, and assist them with extending their freedom of choice and becoming responsible for their behavior.

To support our school safety initiatives and character education programs, we are able to generate the following teaching and learning objectives from the above goals:

- To develop a framework for placing students in environments that will accentuate their abilities.
- To involve parents in extracurricular activities and training that provide enriching experiences for all family members.
- To develop a curriculum rich in language and provide for language amplification through reading, speaking, writing, listening, and dramatization.
- To provide counseling as needed for both students and parents to help them improve their communication and problem solving skills.
- To design learning activities that promote students' creative and critical thinking as well as their affective and ethical sensibilities.
- To train teachers and parents in ways to provide an open and nurturing environment that enhances the emerging gifts and talents of their students and children.

We must remember that children learn all the time and quite naturally. We can use this knowledge to encourage them to manipulate ideas, examine consequences, and combine different options into solution-alternatives for troubling problems. We can also help them learn by modeling the very behaviors we are teaching—modeling positive, growth-producing behaviors is the best way to teach children. We say more by what we do than by the words we use.

Interacting with children, planning for discovery experiences, including them in adult conversations, and asking them questions that are non-threatening and open-ended allow for responses that are creative and fluid (they take into consideration age and ability differences). Open-ended questions and dialogue that are non-punitive and non-directive encourage critical judgment, voicing different perspectives on issues, and thoughtful deliberation.

BUILDING RELATIONSHIPS AND RESOLVING CONFLICTS

An additional strategy used in school safety and character education programs is training students, parents, and teachers in the skills of conflict resolution. Conflicts occur between people when the behavior of one person interferes in some way with the actions of another person. School safety programs usually target students with potential violent and disruptive behaviors, and students who have already displayed these behaviors. Preventive measures, to be effective, begin early and school all children in strategies for building and maintaining friendships and in resolving conflicts in a win-win fashion. Additionally, many school safety programs train families in these methods as well.

To build positive relationships with others, children need to understand why people like each other. Research tells us that we:

- Like people who are pleasant rather than unpleasant,
- Like those who agree with us more than those who always disagree with us,
- Like those who like us more than those who dislike us,
- Like those who cooperate with us more than those who compete with us,
- Like those who praise us more than those who criticize us,
- Like those whose behavior provides us with maximum reward at a minimum cost,
- Like those who do not try to manipulate us, and
- Like those who do us favors, but we don't like people whose favors seem to have strings attached.[16]

A sound character education program will teach children how to take responsibility for their own behaviors and for the welfare of their friends, including the significant adults in their lives. Self-understanding is essential to relationship building. This value is the most satisfactory answer to the current alienation and anomie that is felt by children and families, teenagers, and perhaps teachers who many times feel isolated in their classrooms. We live in a highly industrialized, technological, and impersonal society, one that seemingly has no definable ethic. Students in particular feel anxiety in schools that seem to diminish the personal in place of a compilation of statistics, test scores, and labels that are supposed to define who they are.

One problem for character educators and for those seeking to minimize violence in their schools and homes is how to satisfy a person's basic need for full and valued participation in families, schools, churches, and other institutions that are esteemed in our society. We all seek meaning and purpose in our lives. We need to feel that we are useful and necessary to someone or some cause. Self-understanding involves clarifying, identifying, and committing ourselves to values and beliefs that will direct our lives in meaningful ways. Once a commitment has been made, new experiences will cause us to visit, over and over again, the self-evaluation process.

Self-understanding is the foundation stone of building positive, growth producing relationships with others. Productive individuals must have the emotional stability to confront continuous change and the necessary skills to engage in an ongoing process of personal identity seeking and problem solving. Here is where parents and teachers play such an important role. They need to understand the benefits of exercising critical judgment and asking questions. Like us, children have difficulty dealing with change. As they seek self-understanding and the wherewithal to build positive relationships with others, we can assist them by modeling reason, intelligence, and a fair-minded disposition, including the selection of appropriate strategies and behaviors that build lasting friendships and are able to bring resolution to troubling problems.

The skills needed for resolving conflicts are built on self-understanding and our ability to create and sustain lasting friendships. But, no matter how hard we try, conflicts occur. Even if we are able to control what we say and do, we cannot control what others say and do. We get upset, angry, and sometimes say and do things that cause additional conflicts. Therefore, character education and school safety programs will build within their strategies a training component that focuses on conflict resolution. Techniques abound in conflict resolution,[17] but we should keep in mind the following key values which can form a foundation for settling our difficulties in ethical and honorable ways:

- Sensitivity to others and to the environment,
- The ability to discover the complexities of situations,
- Creativity and imagination that allows us to "see" new possibilities,
- A willingness to learn from experience,
- Fairness and objectivity in judging and evaluating other people and different situations, and
- The courage to change when needed.

In summary, when focusing on building relationships and resolving conflicts, we need to remember the words of John Dewey, who tells us that the school is primarily a social institution and that education is the fundamental method of social progress and reform.[18] Education, at home and at school, is the process of coming to share in a wider social consciousness. The subjects we study have lasted as basic educational disciplines because they discipline the character, the will, and behavior. Experience has informed us that character is simply habit long continued. Our responsibility is to introduce children to a menu of good habits and instill in them a respect for life, all life.

BUILDING CHARACTER THROUGH SERVICE

Dr. Philip F. Vincent, in his book *Developing Character in Students,* has designed a character education program with what he calls "five spokes":

1. Rules and Procedures,
2. Cooperative Learning,
3. Teaching for Thinking,
4. Reading for Character, and
5. Service Learning.[19]

The emphasis in this section is on "service learning," the fifth of Vincent's five spokes. He says, "In my travels around the country, I continually find students and teachers working together in service projects ranging from food drives to assisting individuals seriously impacted by natural or personal disasters. When I ask them about their service experiences, nearly all students respond that they are/were positive experiences. Some cited personal or moral growth as an outcome. Others said that serving others is practicing what the Bible demands. Still others describe how they felt better about themselves after serving others. All of these responses have been shown to be attributed to service learning."

In their report, "High School Community Service: A Review of Research and Programs," Conrad and Hedin found that service learning helps promote the following:

- Self-esteem,
- Personal efficacy (sense of worth and competence),
- Ego and moral development,
- Exploration of new roles, identities, and interests,
- Willingness to take risks, accept new challenges,
- Revised and reinforced values and beliefs, and
- Taking responsibility for and accepting consequences of one's own actions.[20]

Service leaning enhances character education and school safety programs in the following ways:

- Service learning makes abstract moral principles concrete and real,
- Self-worth is gained by the emotional satisfaction gained from helping others and from completing a "job well done,"
- Service learning supports the development of such values as self-discipline and fidelity to a commitment,
- Participating in service learning activities changes youngsters and moves them in a positive direction—it builds character.[21]

Other educators who are experts in character education agree that community service projects offer powerful learning opportunities for students and their families. Vincent agrees and concludes, "The first question a school staff must ask itself is, 'Is this a school where we are truly caring toward our students?' In other words, does the staff welcome the students daily and outwardly show that they care about them? The students will not adopt a caring attitude toward others unless they feel they themselves are cared about."

In Conclusion

This chapter has taken the suggestions of national researchers on school safety and provided the parameters of a character education program that includes many of the long-term strategies that they suggest. Dr. E. Paul Torrance tells a story about Dr. Ruth Dalbeck that is worth repeating here.[22] He says that Dr. Dalbeck was an elementary school teacher who was about to give up teaching. Discipline was so bad and difficult that she could not teach for taking care of the many problems in her room. She finally devised a solution that solved the problem, and wrote about it in her book, *I'll Take the Sun*. The subtitle of the book is *Conflict Resolution and Image Building in the Classroom and With Families*. Her solution was simple and creative. She calls it Conflict, Criticism, and Solution (CCS Method) in which the children in her class are involved in solving their own problems and resolving their own conflicts. The children in the class loved it and asked for this special time each day. Torrance concludes, "While Dr. Dalbeck's procedure is a simple one, it takes training and courage." This is the message that educators need to hear as they set about building school safety and character education programs in their schools.

6

National Resources for Safe School Programs

Organizations, Alliances, Centers, and Professional Development Groups

AmericanSchoolSafety.com is a Core Group of Security Professionals providing services to the educational community:
http://www.americanschoolsafety.com/program.html

Center for Effective Collaboration and Practice
http://cecp.air.org/about.htm

It is the mission of the Center for Effective Collaboration and Practice to support and promote a reoriented national preparedness to foster the development and the adjustment of children with, or at risk of developing, serious emotional disturbances. To achieve that goal, the Center is dedicated to a policy of collaboration at federal, state, and local levels that contributes to and facilitates the production, exchange, and use of knowledge about effective practices.

Center for the Prevention of School Violence (CPSV)
North Carolina State University
c/o Dr. Pamela L. Riley, Executive Director
20 Enterprise Street, Suite 2, Raleigh, NC 27607-7375
Toll Free: 800-299-6054, Phone: 919-515-9397, Fax: 919-515-9561
Web: http://www.ncsu.edu/cpsv

CPSV serves as a clearinghouse for information on the problem of school violence. In addition to developing school violence prevention programs and conducting related research, CPSV maintains a resource library and responds to information requests. CPSV's Web site lists special projects, events, and publications related to school violence.

Center for the Study and Prevention of Violence (CSPV)
Institute of Behavioral Science
University of Colorado at Boulder, Campus Box 442
Boulder, CO 80309-0442
Phone: 303-492-8465, Fax: 303-443-3297
E-mail: cspv@colorado.edu
Web: http://www.colorado.edu/cspv

CSPV provides assistance to groups that are committed to understanding and preventing violence, particularly adolescent violence. It conducts research on the causes of violence and on the efficacy of prevention and intervention programs, collects related literature, offers technical assistance on the evaluation and development of violence prevention programs, and provides direct information services to the public through access to customized databases that can be searched by topic area. CSPV's Web site includes information on model prevention programs and links to databases of violence-related information.

Children's Safety Network (CSN)
National Injury and Violence Prevention Resource Center
Education Development Center, Inc.
55 Chapel Street, Newton, MA 02458-1060
Phone: 617-969-7101, ext. 2207, Fax: 617-244-3436
E-mail: *csn@edc.org*
Web: http://www.edc.org/HHD/csn/index.html

CSN provides resources and technical assistance to maternal and child health agencies and other organizations seeking to reduce unintentional injuries and violence to children and adolescents. CSN's Web site includes a variety of resources on school safety and violence prevention, as well as links to other injury prevention Web sites.

Conflict Resolution Education Network (CREnet)

1527 New Hampshire Avenue, NW, Washington, DC 20036
Phone: 202-667-9700, Fax: 202-667-8629
E-mail: *nidr@crenet.org*
Web: http://www.crenet.org

CREnet (formerly the National Institute for Dispute Resolution and the National Association for Mediation in Education) is the primary national and international clearinghouse for information, resources, and technical assistance in the field of conflict resolution education. It promotes the development, implementation, and institutionalization of school- and university-based conflict resolution programs and curricula. CREnet's Web site includes a list of conflict resolution programs and practitioners.

Girls Incorporated National Headquarters

120 Wall Street, Third Floor, New York, NY 10005
Phone: 212-509-2000, Fax: 212-509-8708
E-mail: *girlsincorporated@girls-inc.org*
Web: http://www.girlsinc.org

Girls Incorporated is a national youth organization dedicated to helping every girl become strong, smart, and bold. Girls Incorporated develops research-based informal education programs that encourage girls to take risks and master physical, intellectual, and emotional challenges. Major programs address math and science education, pregnancy prevention, media literacy, adolescent health, substance-abuse prevention, and sports participation.

Institute on Violence and Destructive Behavior (IVDB)

1265 University of Oregon, Eugene, OR 97403-1265
Phone: 541-346-3592
E-mail: *ivdb@darkwing.uoregon.edu*
Web: http://interact.uoregon.edu/ivdb/ivdb.html

IVDB studies the conditions and factors relating to the development and prevention of violence among children and adolescents. In addition, IVDB provides training and technical assistance to schools, families, and community members. IVDB's Web site includes information on projects and grants, outreach and prevention programs, and school safety planning.

National Alliance for Safe Schools
http://www.safeschools.org/
School violence is not only an urban problem. Today, all schools must have an active plan for creating and maintaining a healthy and safe environment for students and faculty.

**National Association of School Safety and
Law Enforcement Officials**
http://www.nassleo.org/

National Criminal Justice Reference Service (NCJRS)
P.O. Box 6000, Rockville, MD 20849-6000
Toll Free: 800-851-3420, Phone: 301-519-5500
TTY: 877-712-9279
E-mail: *askncjrs@ncjrs.org*
Web: http://www.ncjrs.org
NCJRS is one of the most extensive sources of information on criminal and juvenile justice in the world, providing services to an international community of policymakers and professionals. Funded by the U.S. Department of Justice (DOJ), NCJRS maintains an online database of abstracts of more than 145,000 criminal justice books, journal articles, and reports published by DOJ; local, state, and other federal government agencies; international organizations; and the private sector.

National Education Association (NEA) Safe Schools Home Page
http://www.nea.org/issues/safescho
Statements, publications, and advice from the NEA.

**National Mental Health and Education Center for Children and
Families Safe School Resources**
http://www.naspcenter.org/safe_schools/safeschools.htm
A public service program of the National Association of School Psychologists. The Center has resources available to help parents and teachers deal with school violence, including developing a crisis response plan: Guidelines for School Personnel and Helping Children Cope with a Disaster.

National Resource Center for Safe Schools (NRCSS)
Northwest Regional Educational Laboratory
101 SW Main, Suite 500, Portland, OR 97204
Toll Free: 800-268-2275, Phone: 503-275-0131
Fax: 503-275-0444
E-mail: *safeschools@nwrel.org*
Web: http://www.safetyzone.org

NRCSS, which is funded by the U.S. Department of Education, works with schools, communities, state and local education agencies, and other concerned individuals and agencies to create safe learning environments and prevent school violence. Visitors to the NRCSS Web site can access a resource database, review promising programs, and request copies of publications related to school safety planning, violence prevention, conflict resolution, and substance-abuse prevention.

National School Safety and Security Services
http://www.schoolsecurity.org/

A Cleveland (Ohio)–based, national consulting firm specializing in school security and crisis preparedness training, security assessments, and related safety consulting for K–12 schools, law enforcement, and other youth safety providers. Web site pulls together information on this issue.

National School Safety Center (NSSC)
141 Duesenberg Drive, Suite 11, Westlake Village, CA 91362
Phone: 805-373-9977, Fax: 805-373-9277
E-mail: *info@nssc1.org*
Web: http://www.nssc1.org

NSSC advocates for the prevention of school crime and violence by providing information and resources and identifying strategies and promising programs that support safe schools worldwide. NSSC's Web site includes descriptions of related publications, products, services, training, seminars, and resources for parents and educators.

National Youth Gang Center (NYGC)
Institute for Intergovernmental Research
P.O. Box 12729, Tallahassee, FL 32317
Phone: 850-385-0600, Fax: 850-386-5356

E-mail: *nygc@iir.com*
Web: http://www.iir.com/nygc

NYGC works to increase and maintain the body of knowledge on youth gangs and effective responses to them. It assists state and local jurisdictions in the collection, analysis, and exchange of information on gang-related demographics, legislation, literature, research, and promising program strategies. It also coordinates the activities of the U.S. Department of Justice's Office of Juvenile Justice and Delinquency Prevention Youth Gang Consortium.

National Youth Violence Resource Center
    http://www.safeyouth.org/directory/dir2.htm
    Directory of Topics A–Z.

Office of Juvenile Justice and Delinquency Prevention (OJJDP)
    U.S. Department of Justice
    810 Seventh Street, NW, Washington, DC 20531
    Phone: 202-307-5911, Fax: 202-307-2093
    E-mail: *askjj@ojp.usdoj.gov*
    Web: http://ojjdp.ncjrs.org

OJJDP provides national leadership, coordination, and resources to develop, implement, and support effective methods to prevent juvenile victimization and to respond appropriately to juvenile delinquency. OJJDP's Web site lists related grants, publications, and links to other OJJDP programs.

Partnerships Against Violence Network (PAVNET) Online
    http://www.pavnet.org

PAVNET Online is a virtual library of information on violence and at-risk youth. It contains data from seven federal agencies, including the U.S. Department of Education, the U.S. Department of Justice, and the U.S. Department of Health and Human Services.

Safe and Drug-Free Schools Program (SDFSP)
    U.S. Department of Education
    Portals Building, 600 Independence Avenue, SW
    Washington, DC 20202

E-mail: *safeschl@ed.gov*
Web: http://www.ed.gov/offices/OESE/SDFS

SDFSP is the federal government's primary vehicle for reducing drug, alcohol, and tobacco use, as well as violence, through education and prevention activities in the schools. SDFSP's Web site includes related information on publications, grants, research, and model programs.

Safe School Model Home Page

http://www.safeschoolmodel.org/index.html

The Moderator's Column invites a cultural transformation of our social system. The Findings page of the site contains information on identified causes of school violence. The Public-Private Partnership Model provides suggested major areas of concentration to resolve these problems nonviolently. The School Shooting page is introduced to create a sense of urgency. The archive provides various links on research findings, successful models, and information on scholarship money and grants so that visiting this site can benefit the readers.

ERIC Resources

ERIC (Educational Resources Information Center) is the U.S. Department of Education's nationwide information network that provides ready access to education literature. The ERIC system centers on the world's largest education database, which contains a wealth of information on school safety, violence prevention, and other topics. The database can be searched online and in many libraries. For general information about ERIC, contact ACCESS ERIC, the reference and referral component of the ERIC system.

ACCESS ERIC

Toll Free: 800-LET-ERIC (538-3742)
Phone: 301-519-5157, Fax: 301-519-6760
E-mail: *accesseric@accesseric.org*
Web: http://www.eric.ed.gov/

In addition, the clearinghouses listed below offer specific information on topics related to school safety and violence prevention.

ERIC Clearinghouse on Counseling and Student Services
Toll Free: 800-414-9769, Phone: 336-334-4114
E-mail: *ericcass@uncg.edu*
Web: http://www.uncg.edu/edu/ericcass

ERIC Clearinghouse on Educational Management
Toll Free: 800-438-8841, Phone: 541-346-5043
E-mail: *ppiele@oregon.uoregon.edu*
Web: http://eric.uoregon.edu

ERIC Clearinghouse on Urban Education
Toll Free: 800-601-4868, Phone: 212-678-3433
E-mail: *eric-cue@columbia.edu*
Web: http://eric-web.tc.columbia.edu

National Clearinghouse for Educational Facilities
(Affiliate ERIC Clearinghouse)
Toll Free: 888-552-0624, Phone: 202-289-7800
E-mail: *ncef@nibs.org*
Web: http://www.cdfacilities.org

Selected State Government Resources

The Center for Safe Schools and the
Pennsylvania Department of Education
http://www.center-school.org/viol_prev/css/toolkit.htm

The Center for Safe Schools and the Pennsylvania Department of Education have developed a "Toolkit for School Safety Planning" which was sent to every school district, intermediate unit and vocational technical school in Pennsylvania. The toolkit is intended to serve as a desktop reference for school safety and violence prevention resources. This resource was provided in a three ring binder format so that schools could add updated information from the Department of Education in the future and customize the binder to fit their needs by including local policies, press clippings, laws and resources. Over 40 different resources were included in the binder.

Georgia Toll-free School Safety Hotline
http://www.doe.k12.ga.us/federal/hotlinebackground.html

Georgia and federal laws relating to school safety. It is part of the Title IV Safe & Drug-Free Schools Program.

Indiana School Safety Specialist Academy,
Indiana Department of Education
http://ideanet.doe.state.in.us/isssa/websites.html

School safety programs, resources and related websites.

Kentucky Center for School Safety (CSS)
http://www.corrections.eku.edu/css.htm

The Kentucky Center for School Safety is mandated by 1998 legislation and represents a collaborative effort between Eastern Kentucky University, Murray State University, the University of Kentucky, and the Kentucky School Boards Association. CSS is a central point for dissemination of information about successful school safety programs. The center also works with schools, justice system agencies, related human service organizations, and communities to coordinate training, technical assistance, and analysis of data related to school safety issues. Since the inception of CSS, department faculties have worked closely with CSS staff to accomplish these tasks; one member of the department holds a School Safety Research Fellowship.

The New York State Center for School Safety
Phone: 845-255-8989

The New York State Center for School Safety (formerly the Upstate Center for School Safety) works with schools across the state preparing to implement the state's SAVE (Safe Schools Against Violence in Education) Legislation. In addition to the SAVE Legislation, the Center has been busy with many new initiatives, and continues to offer training and technical assistance to schools on planning a safer school environment.

It serves as a resource to the NYS Attorney General's Office (http://www.oag.state.ny.us/) on the implementation of the SAVI (Students Against Violence Initiative), a student-based project in 11 schools focusing on reducing violence and harassing behaviors.

It also collaborates with Cornell University and the University of Rochester on the NYS Department of Health funded ACT for Youth initiative (http://www.health.state.ny.us/home.html). This initiative focuses on positive youth development as a means to reduce violence and risky sexual behavior.

Planning and Design for K–12 School Facilities in North Carolina

http://www.schoolclearinghouse.org/

The School Planning Section of the North Carolina Department of Public Instruction assists North Carolina school districts, architects and designers in the planning and design of high quality school facilities that enhance education and provide lasting value to the children and citizens of the state. Major areas of concentration include school renovation, IDEA and technology grants, what to do in the case of bomb threats, the Prototype School Design Clearinghouse, school facilities information, planning assistance, publications and workshops, and The State Bond for Public School Facility Needs.

Virginia Center for School Safety

http://www.vaschoolsafety.com/

The Virginia Center for School Safety is a comprehensive resource center for information and research about school safety in the Commonwealth. The Center, which is housed at the Department of Criminal Justice Services, was created in April 2000 by Virginia General Assembly's passage of HB 391 (§9–173.21). Its mission is multi-faceted and includes training for educators in identifying and helping at-risk students, distributing information on current laws and effective school safety initiatives, collecting and distributing school safety data, and facilitating new initiatives involving the public and private sectors.

Publications Related to School and Youth Violence

Annual Report On School Safety (1st, 1998)

http://www.ed.gov/pubs/AnnSchoolRept98/index.html
http://www.ed.gov/PDFDocs/schoolsafety.pdf

Following the tragic shooting at West Paducah High School in

December 1997, President Clinton directed the U.S. Departments of Education and Justice to prepare, for the first time, an annual report on school safety. The first report provides parents, schools, and communities with an overview of the scope of school crime, and describes actions schools and communities can take to address this critical issue.

Annual Report on School Safety (2nd, 1999)
http://www.ed.gov/PDFDocs/InterimAR.pdf

Updated description of the nature and extent of crime and violence on school property. Describes measures some schools have taken to prevent and address school violence.

Annual Report on School Safety (3rd, 2000)
http://www.safetyzone.org/pdf/schoolsafety3.pdf

Highlights the nature and scope of school violence by examining data on issues such as homicides and suicides at school, crimes against students and teachers, student perceptions of school safety, and school discipline.

Approaches to School Safety in America's Largest Cities
http://www.vera.org/publication_pdf/apprchs_school_safety.pdf

A report by Melorra Sochet of the Vera Institute of Justice. Prepared for the New York State Governor's Task Force on School Safety in the summer of 1999, "Approaches to School Safety in America's Largest Cities" shows the ways in which school systems and state and local governments in New York, Los Angeles, Chicago, Houston and Philadelphia structure their institutions to address school safety. Much of the report was later incorporated into the Task Force's final report and recommendations, which were endorsed by the Governor and released to the public in October 1999. 60pp.

Appropriate and Effective Use of Security Technologies in U.S. Schools
http://magic.lib.msu.edu/search/t?SEARCH=Appropriate+and+Effective+Use+of+Security+Technologies+
http://www.energy.gov/HQDocs/schoolsecurity/pdf.htm

This guide for schools and law enforcement agencies reviews such security measures as video surveillance cameras and metal detectors, their costs, strengths and weaknesses, and legal issues that may be involved in their use. This document is also available in the MSU Main Library Government Documents stacks.

Centers for Disease Control and Prevention/ Center for Injury Prevention and Control
http://www.cdc.gov/ncipc/dvp/bestpractices.htm

"Best Practices of Youth Violence Prevention: A Sourcebook for Community Action."

Classroom Killers? Hallway Hostages? How Schools Can Prevent and Manage School Crises (Book Description)
http://www.schoolsecurity.org/crisis-book.html

Combating Fear and Restoring Safety in Schools (NCJ 167888)
http://www.ncjrs.org/pdffiles/167888.pdf

This 16-page bulletin was written by June L. Arnette, Communications Director, and Marjorie C. Walsleben, Communications Specialist, at the National School Safety Center. The bulletin addresses manifestations of street violence that have encroached on schools: bullying, gangs, the possession and use of weapons, substance abuse, and violence in the community. It also describes strategies and programs that are being implemented by concerned citizens to restore safety and calm to their schools. Contacts for further information are provided.

Creating Safe and Drug-Free Schools: An Action Guide
http://www.ncjrs.org/

For the user's convenience, this document is also available in Portable Document Format (331K) from the National Criminal Justice Reference System (NCJRS). To view the pdf version, you will need a copy of the Adobe Acrobat Reader. If you do not have Acrobat, you can download a free copy from Adobe.

Crime in the Schools: Reducing Conflict with Student Problem Solving
http://www.ojp.usdoj.gov/nij/pubs-sum/177618.htm

Teachers, administrators, and students are expressing increasing concerns about the presence of drugs, gangs, weapons and crime on school campuses. This NIJ Research in Brief, titled Crime in the Schools: Reducing Conflict With Student Problem Solving, discusses an investigation of a student-based problem-solving model for reducing crime in the nation's schools. Results of this study indicate that a guided group process can reduce school crime and improve the overall school climate. However, most of the conflicts uncovered during this project concerned everyday school interactions rather than gangs, drugs, and armed agitators.

Crime Time Bomb

http://www.usnews.com/usnews/issue/crime.htm

Rising juvenile crime, and predictions that it is going to get worse, are prodding cities, states and Congress to seek a balance between tougher laws and preventive measures. *U.S. News* Online article.

Criminal Justice Resources

"School Safety and Violence."
http://www.lib.msu.edu/harris23/crimjust/school.htm

Early Warning, Timely Response: A Guide to Safe Schools

http://www.ed.gov/offices/OSERS/OSEP/earlywrn.html

A report that provides an overview of research-based practices, including: characteristics of a safe and responsive school; early warning signs; getting help for troubled children; developing a prevention and responsive plan; and dealing with a crisis. The guide was developed by the U.S. Department of Education and Department of Justice.

ERIC Clearinghouse on Counseling and Student Services (ERIC CASS)

Virtual Library Reading Room, "Bullying in Schools."
http://ericcass.uncg.edu/virtuallib/bullying/bullyingbook.html

ERIC Clearinghouse on Counseling and Student Services (ERIC CASS)

Virtual Library Reading Room, "School Violence."
http://ericcass.uncg.edu/virtuallib/violence/violencebook.html

Exposure to Violence and Victimization at School
http://iume.tc.columbia.edu/choices/briefs/choices04.html

Facts About Violence Among Youth and Violence in Schools
http://www.cdc.gov/od/oc/media/fact/violence.htm

By Daniel J. Flannery, Institute for the Study and Prevention of Violence, Kent State University, and Mark I. Singer, Mandel School of Applied Social Sciences, Case Western Reserve University. Institute for Urban and Minority Education, Teachers College, Columbia University, Choices Brief no. 4, 1999.

Federal Activities Addressing Violence in Schools
http://www.cdc.gov/nccdphp/dash/violence/

Identifies all ongoing and recently completed projects that either directly address the problem of violence that occurs on school property, around school, or at school-associated events, or indirectly address the problem of school violence by focusing on precursors of violence, factors associated with violence, or mechanisms for preventing violent behavior. For each project, the inventory provides information on the lead or funding agency and collaborating federal agencies and non-federal partners and provides contact information for federal agency staff.

Governor's Columbine Review Commission Report
http://www.state.co.us/columbine/
May 2001.

Gun Violence in Schools
http://www.abanet.org/gunviol/schoolshm.html

Access the ABA's policy, background report, congressional correspondence and facts on gun violence in schools.

How Can We Prevent Violence in Our Schools
http://www.accesseric.org/resources/parent/prevent.html

Despite heightened public attention following a surge in multiple homicides in schools, overall school crime rates are declining, according to the new 1999 Annual Report on School Safety (U.S.

Department of Education and U.S. Department of Justice, 1999). This brochure offers an overview of current school-safety and violence-prevention issues and recommends organizations and resources that can provide additional information.

In the Spotlight: School Safety

> http://www.ncjrs.org/school_safety/school_safety.html

"In the Spotlight" is a new bi-monthly feature that focuses on prevalent issues in crime, public safety, and drug policy. This issue provides information about bullying, conflict resolution, security planning and other key issues. Also provides news about training and technical assistance programs, publications, and facts and figures.

Indicators of School Crime and Safety, 1998

> http://nces.ed.gov/pubsearch/pubsinfo.asp?pubid=98251

This report, the first in a series of annual reports on school crime and safety from the Bureau of Justice Statistics and the National Center for Education Statistics, presents the latest available data on school crime and student safety. The report provides a profile of school crime and safety in the United States and describes the characteristics of the victims of these crimes. It is organized as a series of indicators, with each indicator presenting data on different aspects of school crime and safety. There are five sections to the report: Nonfatal Student Victimization—Student Reports; Violence and Crime at School—Public School Principal/Disciplinarian Reports; Violent Deaths at School; Nonfatal Teacher Victimization at School—Teacher Reports; and School Environment. Each section contains a set of indicators that, taken as a whole, describe a distinct aspect of school crime and safety.

Indicators of School Crime and Safety, 1999

> http://nces.ed.gov/pubsearch/pubsinfo.asp?pubid=1999057

Analyzes national data from several sources on crimes committed in schools and to and from schools. In addition, "data for crime away from school are also presented to place school crime in the context of crime in the larger society." According to the NCES, this report represents the most current detailed statistical information on the nature of crime in schools. Source: Scout Report, October 1, 1999.

Indicators of School Crime and Safety, 2000
 http://nces.ed.gov/pubsearch/pubsinfo.asp?pubid=2001017

This report presents data on crime at school from the perspectives of students, teachers, principals, and the general population from an array of sources that include: the National Crime Victimization Survey (1992–98); the School Crime Supplement to the National Crime Victimization Survey (1989, 1995 and 1999); the Youth Risk Behavior Survey (1993, 1995, and 1997); and, the School and Staffing Survey (1993–94). A joint effort by the Bureau of Justice Statistics and the National Center for Education Statistics, the report examines crime occurring in school as well as on the way to and from school. Data for crime away from school are also presented to place school crime in the context of crime in the larger society. The report provides the most current detailed statistical information to inform the nation on the nature of crime in schools.

Indicators of School Crime and Safety, 2001
 http://www.ojp.usdoj.gov/bjs/abstract/iscs01.htm

NCJ190075. Between 1992 and 1999, violent victimization rates at schools generally declined from 48 crimes per 1,000 students ages 12 through 18 to 33 per 1,000 students. 191pp.

Keep Schools Safe
 http://www.keepschoolssafe.org/

On September 2, 1998, the National Association of Attorneys General and the National School Boards Association joined together to address the escalating problem of youth violence occurring across our country. This Youth Violence and School Safety Initiative is dedicated to promoting a mutual response to violent instances occurring in communities and schools.

Keeping Children Safe in School: A Resource for States
 http://www.childrensdefense.org/publications/schoolviolence.html

This report by the Children's Defense Fund is designed to give you the latest facts on school violence and some useful information on how to make schools in your community safer. From conflict resolution to after-school programs, this guide will provide you with the tools to learn about these successful school violence prevention initiatives. This handy guide has contact names, numbers, and web sites of key organizations where you can obtain helpful fact sheets, resource material, and program information.

Kids These Days: What Americans Really Think About the Younger Generation
http://www.publicagenda.org/specials/kids/kids.htm

Michigan Electronic Library School Violence & Safety Page
http://mel.org/education/edu-safety.html

National Evaluation of the Safe Schools/ Healthy Students Initiative
http://www.ojjdp.ncjrs.org/grants/safeschool/intro.html

The U.S. Departments of Justice, Education, and Health and Human Services (Agencies) are requesting applications for a national evaluation of the Safe Schools/Healthy Students Initiative. The overarching goal of the evaluation is to document the effectiveness of collaborative community efforts to promote safe schools and provide opportunities for healthy childhood development. The evaluation will demonstrate how community collaborative efforts develop, function, and facilitate change within community institutions and within individuals.

National Institute of Justice
http://www.ojp.usdoj.gov/nij/newsletter/0499chapter.html

"Youth Violence in America" by Mark H. Moore and Michael Tonry.

Nuts and Bolts of Implementing School Safety Programs
http://www.vera.org/PDF/nutsbolts.pdf

A report by Melorra Sochet and Catherine Berryman for the Vera Institute of Justice. The report is intended to help teachers, principals, and school administrators find the right school safety programs. The manual identifies programs from around the country and describes the resources needed to implement each program. 2000.

Office of Special Education Programs (OSEP): "Mission"

http://www.ed.gov/offices/OSERS/OSEP/About/aboutusmission.html

OSEP is dedicated to improving results for infants, toddlers, children and youth with disabilities, ages birth through 21 by providing leadership and financial support to assist states and local districts. OSEP administers the Individuals With Disabilities Education Act (IDEA). IDEA authorizes formula grants to states, and discretionary grants to institutions of higher education and other nonprofit organizations to support research, demonstrations, technical assistance and dissemination, technology and personnel development and parent-training and information centers. These programs are intended to ensure that the rights of infants, toddlers, children, and youth with disabilities and their parents are protected.

Open Directory Project Violence in School Web Links

http://dmoz.org/Society/Issues/Violence/School/

An Overview of Strategies to Reduce School Violence

http://eric-web.tc.columbia.edu/digests/dig115.html

A digest on school violence available through the ERIC Clearinghouse on Urban Education.

Preventing School Violence

http://www.ncjrs.org/txtfiles1/nij/180972.txt
http://www.ncjrs.org/pdffiles1/nij/180972.pdf

In response to recent, tragic instances of violence in our nation's schools, NIJ and other sponsoring Office of Justice Programs bureaus and offices presented a plenary session on school violence at the 1999 Conference on Criminal Justice Research and Evaluation. The three speakers addressed different aspects of school violence prevention. Sociologist Joseph Sheley suggests that youth violence occurs more frequently in students' neighborhoods and that schools are rarely the source of violence as much as they are the sites where disputes arising in the neighborhood are acted out. Sheley also notes that the prime motive for carrying weapons is fear rather than criminal behavior. Ron Prinz argues that prevention must be considered from an empirically based, developmental perspective that also helps parents, teachers, and communities to develop and enforce congruent interventions. Public health psychiatrist Sheppard Kellam uses his decades-long work in Chicago and Baltimore to illustrate the necessity of community involvement when designing prevention programs. NCJ180972.

Preventing School Violence—The Littleton Tragedy
http://www.nydic.org/littleton.html

A compilation of resources by the National Youth Development Information Center.

Preventing Youth Violence in Urban Schools:
An Essay Collection
http://eric-web.tc.columbia.edu/monographs/uds107_index.html

Wendy Schwartz, March 1996.

Promoting Safety in Schools: International Experience and
Action
http://www.ncjrs.org/pdffiles1/bja/186937.pdf
http://www.ncjrs.org/txtfiles1/bja/186937.txt

NCJ 186937 describes the issues of school violence and school safety as concerns seen throughout the world. The document addresses the goals of implementing school safety and having plans to prevent crises and deal with the ones that arise. 68pp.

Protecting Students from Harassment and
Hate Crimes: A Guide for Schools
http://www.ed.gov/pubs/Harassment/

Provides information to help schools and school districts protect students from harassment and hate crimes. This September 1999 guide defines and describes harassment and hate crimes, contains information about applicable laws, details specific positive steps that schools can take to prevent and respond to harassment, includes sample policies and procedures used by school districts in the United States, and identifies many of the resource materials available to assist schools. This version of the document includes recent court decisions.

Response to the Columbine School Incident
      http://www.Colorado.EDU/cspv/Columbine/ColumbineFrame.
htm

      Report and web links put together by the Center for the Study
of Violence, University of Colorado, Boulder.

Safeguarding Our Children: An Action Guide:
  Implementing Early Warning, Timely Response
      http://www.ed.gov/offices/OSERS/OSEP/ActionGuide/

      Helps schools develop and carry out a violence prevention and
response plan that can be customized to fit each school's particular
strengths. This guide presents strategies that schools have used successfully to create and implement violence prevention plans; provides
examples of sound practices and programs; and offers suggestions on
recognizing, reporting, and using early warning signs effectively.

Safer School Resources from the
  Bureau of Justice Administration
      http://www.ojp.usdoj.gov/BJA/html/safe.htm

      Provides links to the following National Crime Prevention Coun-
cil Resources:

  • Stopping School Violence (12 Things You Can Do)
  • Making Safer Schools
  • Strategies for Educators and Law Enforcement to Prevent Vio-
    lence
  • Back-to-School Checklist for Parents
  • How to Start a School Crime Watch
  • Making Peace: Tips for Managing Conflict

School and Community Interventions to
  Prevent Serious and Violent Offending
      http://www.ncjrs.org/html/ojjdp/jjbul9910-1/contents.html

      Although youth who commit serious violent crimes are small in
number, they account for a disproportionate amount of juvenile crime.
How then can we best intervene with this difficult—even dangerous—
population?

School Based Crime Prevention
    http://www.preventingcrime.org/report/chapter5.htm
    Denise Gottfredson. Chapter 5 of "Preventing Crime: What Works, What Doesn't, What's Promising." Courtesy of Preventing Crime.Org.

School House Hype: School Shootings and the Real Risks Kids Face in America
    http://www.cjcj.org/jpi/schoolhouse.html
    Article by Elizabeth Donohue, Vincent Schiraldi, and Jason Ziedenberg, National Center on Juvenile and Criminal Justice.

School Resource Officer Training Program
    http://www.ncjrs.org/pdffiles1/ojjdp/fs200105.pdf
    http://www.ncjrs.org/txtfiles1/ojjdp/fs200105.txt
    Office of Juvenile Justice and Delinquency Prevention Fact Sheet, No. 5, March 2001.

School Shooter: A Threat Assessment Perspective
    http://www.fbi.gov/publications/school/school2.pdf
    Details warning signs in a student's personality, family, school, and social life that could indicate a propensity towards violence. It defines what a threat is and advises school and law enforcement officials on what to do if they suspect someone is at risk for committing a violent act. Courtesy of the FBI.

School Violence: Library of Michigan Bibliography
    http://www.libofmich.lib.mi.us/services/bibs/school.html
    October 2000.

School Violence Resources from the Office of Juvenile Justice and Delinquency Prevention
    http://ojjdp.ncjrs.org/resources/school.html
    A compilation of statements, facts and figures, publications, and information about grants and funding opportunities devoted to the problem of school violence.

School Violence (Special Issue)
   http://www.ncjrs.org/html/ojjdp/jjjournal_2001_6/contents.html
   http://www.ncjrs.org/pdffiles1/ojjdp/188158.pdf

   Juvenile Justice, Vol. 8, No. 1, June 2001, presents three articles that examine the extent and nature of school violence and review promising approaches to creating safe schools and resolving conflicts peacefully; the journal also describes other resources related to these issues.

School Violence: What Is Being Done to
  Combat School Violence? What Should Be Done?
   http://www.access.gpo.gov/congress/house/house07.html

   U.S. Congress. House. Committee on Government Reform. Subcommittee on Criminal Justice, Drug Policy, and Human Resources. Committee Hearing 106–111, May 20, 1999.

Secret Service Working on Early Detection in School Violence
   http://www.publicagenda.org/headlines/headline082400.htm

   The Secret Service is involved in a new project to prevent Columbine-style violence at schools, using the same methods they use to identify potential assassins. Agents from the Secret Service's National Threat Assessment Center, including psychology experts, have examined about 40 recent school shootings and interviewed several of the perpetrators. The final report, which will be made available to police and school officials, will offer suggestions for early detection of potentially threatening students. The report won't contain any profiles of a typical school shooter. "We don't believe in profiles," said Secret Service Director Brian Stafford. "There are no psychological or demographic profiles for the adults who pose threats, and my guess is we're going to find the same thing in children." Instead, the Secret Service focuses on behavior and motives, tracing the shooter's thoughts and actions. One of the project's most useful findings, Stafford said, is that none of the shooters acted "in a spontaneous, impulsive manner." "There's been plenty of time to intervene," he said. "But you have to recognize the signs and have people in place to respond." Public Agenda Online Headline, August 24, 2000.

States Experiment with Schoolhouse Safety
   http://www.stateline.org/story.cfm?storyid=72586
   Article by Tiffany Danitz and John Nagy, April 12, 2000, appearing in Stateline.Org.

The Student Report on School Crime
   http://www.ojp.usdoj.gov/bjs/abstract/srsc.htm
   http://www.ojp.usdoj.gov/bjs/pub/ascii/srsc.txt
   This report is the first focusing on data collected in the 1995 School Crime Supplement (SCS), an enhancement to the National Crime Victimization Survey (NCVS). It compares findings from the 1989 and 1995 SCS on student reports of victimization, drug availability, street gang presence, and gun presence at school. In each year, the SCS was administered to about 10,000 persons age 12 through 19 currently attending school. This report presents the first findings from the 1995 supplement, discussing relationships among the variables examined, such as how drug availability, street gang presence, and gun presence are related to student reports of being victimized at school. April 12, 1998.

Surgeon General's Home Page
   http://www.surgeongeneral.gov/library/youthviolence/toc.html
   "Youth Violence: A Report of the Surgeon General."

The Three Rs and Emergency Preparedness:
   Contingency Planning for our Schools
   http://www.cmsinc.freeservers.com/thethreersandemergencypreparedness.pdf
   Article by Edward V. Badolato, President of Contingency Management Services, Inc. December 1999.

Under Siege: Schools as the New Battleground
   http://www.securitysolutions.com/pubs/ac9907/school/a.html
   Strategies to protect students, staff and facilities. A special supplement to Access Control & Security Systems Integration and American School & University.

**The United States Department of Mental Health and
Human Services—The Center for Mental Health Services**
  http://www.mentalhealth.org/schoolviolence/default.asp

The Safe Schools/Healthy Students Initiative is a grant program designed to develop real-world knowledge about what works best to reduce school violence.

**Violence Among Middle School and High School Students:
Analysis and Implications for Prevention**
  http://www.ncjrs.org/txtfiles/166363.txt

This NIJ Research in Brief presents the results of a study examining violent incidents among at-risk middle and high school students. The study focused not only on the types and frequency of these incidents but also on their dynamics—the locations, the "opening moves," the relationship between disputants, the goals and justifications of the aggressor, the role of third parties, and other factors.

**Violence and Discipline Problems in U.S.
Public Schools: 1996–97 (NCES 98030)**
  http://nces.ed.gov/pubs98/violence/

This report presents findings from the Principal/School Disciplinarian Survey on School Violence commissioned by NCES to obtain current data on school violence and other discipline issues in our nation's public elementary and secondary schools. The survey requested information about (1) the actual number of specific crimes that had occurred at school during the 1996–97 academic year; (2) principals' perceptions about the seriousness of a variety of discipline issues at their schools; (3) the types of disciplinary actions schools took against students for some serious violations; and (4) the kinds of security measures and violence prevention programs that were in place in public schools.

Violence in American Schools
  http://www.colorado.edu/cspv/research/violenceschools.html

In this volume, experts from a range of disciplines use a variety of perspectives, notably those of public health, criminology, ecology, and developmental psychology, to review the latest research on the causes of youth violence in the nation's schools and communities and on school-based interventions that have prevented or reduced it. They describe and evaluate strategies for the prevention and treatment of violence that go beyond punishment and incarceration. The volume offers a new strategy for the problem of youth violence, arguing that the most effective interventions use a comprehensive, multi-disciplinary approach and take into account differences in stages of individual development and involvement in overlapping social contexts, families, peer groups, schools, and neighborhoods. Schoolteachers and administrators can use this book profitably. Provided by the Center for the Study and Prevention of Violence.

Violence in the Schools
http://education.indiana.edu/cas/tt/v2i3/v2i3toc.html

A special edition of *Teacher Talk*, a publication of the Center for Adolescent Studies at the School of Education, Indiana University.

Weapons in School and Zero Tolerance
http://www.abanet.org/crimjust/juvjus/cjweapons.html

An online article by Robert E. Shepherd, Jr. and Anthony J. Demarco appearing in the ABA's *Juvenile Justice*, vol. 11, no. 2, Summer 1996.

Yahoo's Current News about School Violence
http://fullcoverage.yahoo.com/Full_Coverage/US/School_Violence

Yahoo's School Violence Web Links
http://dir.yahoo.com/Society_and_Culture/Crime/Juvenile/School_Violence/

Zero Tolerance, Zero Sense
http://er.lib.msu.edu/ejour.cfm

In the wake of a spate of shootings, school boards are adopting strict policies to crack down on trouble-making students. As a result, good kids, whose behavior would have merited a trip to the principal's office in the past, are being suspended, kicked out of school or even prosecuted. Critics say schools should be innovative rather than inflexible in doling out punishment. Article by Margaret Graham Tebo appearing in *ABA Journal*, April 2000, p. 40+.

Miscellaneous Websites

Digest 115

http://eric-web.tc.columbia.edu/digests/dig115.html

This website gives a detail report of strategies used to reduce school and youth violence.

Measures to Ensure School Safety

http://eric-web.tc.columbia.edu/monographs/uds107/preventing_measures.html

Youth violence in many schools, frequently mirroring the situation in the surrounding community, has reached pandemic proportions. In some communities the situation is so bad that young offenders are being sent to boot camps or "shock incarceration."

National School Safety and Security Services

http://www.schoolsecurity.org/

Provides proactive, cost-effective recommendations for preventing and managing violence, reducing risks and liability, and improving public relations.

National School Safety Center

http://www.nssc1.org/

The National School Safety Center was created by presidential directive in 1984 to meet the growing need for additional training and preparation in the area of school crime and violence prevention.

NEA Issues: Safe Schools Home Page

http://www.nea.org/issues/safescho/

What are National Education Association members across the country doing to make all students safe? The Safe Schools section of the NEA Web site puts you in touch with experts and solutions. You'll find out what you can do about school violence and discover resources for children.

Safe and Drug Free Schools Program

http://www.ed.gov/offices/OESE/SDFS/

The Safe and Drug-Free Schools Program is the federal government's primary vehicle for reducing drug, alcohol and tobacco use, and violence, through education and prevention activities in our nation's schools.

Safe Schools for the 21st Century
http://www.s21c-detroit.org/

Explores the principal issues surrounding school violence, the many factors that cause school-based crime, the methods that are being used to prevent violence, and the theoretical constructs on which these programs are based and evaluated.

School Safety Professionals, LLC
http://www.school-safety.com/school2.htm

Offers training materials, plans, policies, procedures and all other work to reflect the issues and problems of individual clients. See also: "The Essential School Safety Guide for Superintendents, Principals, and School Safety Professionals" (1998) at *http://www.school-safety.com/essentia.htm.*

Welcome to Keep Schools Safe
http://msn.directhit.com/msn/search.php?cmd=qry&qry=school+safety. Also: http://www.keepschoolssafe.org/

Featured topics include School Safety Resources, Handling Crisis Situations, What Students Can Do, How Parents Can Get Involved, Model Approaches to School Safety, and Discipline Codes that Work.

Appendix

Resources for the Surgeon General's Report

The following are resources used by the U.S. Surgeon General's Office for its 1999 report on youth violence and some programs and strategies that have been effective in addressing the problem.

Andrews, D. A. (1994, unpublished manuscript). An overview of treatment effectiveness: Research and clinical principles.

____, Zinger, I., Hoge, R. D., Bonta, J., Gendreau, P., & Cullen, F. T. (1990). A clinically relevant and psychologically informed meta-analysis. *Criminology, 28,* 369–387.

Aniskiewicz, R. E., & Wysong, E. E. (1990). Evaluating DARE: Drug education and the multiple meanings of success. *Policy Studies Review, 9,* 727–747.

Aos, S., Phipps, P. V., Barnoski, R., & Leib, R. (1999). *The comparative costs and benefits of programs to reduce crime: A review of national research findings with implications for Washington state* (Report No. 99–05–1202). Olympia, WA: Washington State Institute for Public Policy. [Also available on the World Wide Web: http://www.wsipp.wa.gov/crime/costben.html]

Arbuthnot, J., & Gordon, D. A. (1986). Behavioral and cognitive effects of a moral reasoning development intervention for high-risk behavior-disordered adolescents. *Journal of Consulting and Clinical Psychology, 54,* 208–216.

Bishop, D. (2000). Juvenile offenders in the adult criminal justice system. In M. Tonry (Ed.), *Youth violence. Crime and justice: A review of research* (Vol. 27, pp. 81–168). Chicago: University of Chicago Press.

____, & Frazier, C. (2000). The consequences of waiver. In J. Fagan & F. E. Zimring (Eds.), *The changing borders of juvenile justice: Transfer of adolescents to the criminal court* (pp. 227–276). Chicago: University of Chicago Press.

Boudouris, J., & Turnbull, B. W. (1985). Shock probation in Iowa. *Journal of Offender Counseling, Services and Rehabilitation, 9,* 53–67.

Bry, B. H. (1982). Reducing the incidence of adolescent problems through preventive intervention: One- and five-year follow-up. *American Journal of Community Psychology, 10,* 265–276.

____, & George, F. E. (1980). The preventive effects of early intervention on the attendance and grades of urban adolescents. *Professional Psychology, 2,* 252–260.

_____, & _____ (1979). Evaluating and improving prevention programs: A strategy from drug abuse. *Evaluation and Program Planning*, 2, 127–136.

Buckner, J. C., & Chesney-Lind, M. (1983). Dramatic cures for juvenile crime: An evaluation of a prison-run delinquency prevention program. *Criminal Justice and Behavior*, 10, 227–247.

Center for Substance Abuse Prevention. (2000). CSAP's model programs. Available on the World Wide Web: http://www.samhsa.gov/csap/modelprograms/default.htm

Center for the Study and Prevention of Violence. (1998). *CSPV position summary: D.A.R.E. Program.* Available on the World Wide Web: http://www.colorado.edu/cspv/positions/position3.html

Chamberlain, P., & Mihalic, S. F. (1998). Multi-dimensional treatment foster care. In D. S. Elliott (Series Ed.), *Blueprints for violence prevention. Multi-dimensional treatment foster care.* Boulder, CO: Center for the Study and Prevention of Violence, Institute of Behavioral Sciences, University of Colorado at Boulder.

Chandler, M. J. (1993). Egocentrism and antisocial behavior: The assessment and training of social perspective-taking skills. *Developmental Psychology*, 9, 326–332.

Cohen, P. A., Kulik, J. A., & Kulik, C. L. (1982). Educational outcomes of tutoring: A meta-analysis of findings. *American Educational Research Journal*, 19, 237–248.

Dejong, W. (1987). A short-term evaluation of Project DARE (Drug Abuse Resistance Education): Preliminary indicators of effectiveness. *Journal of Drug Education*, 17, 279–294.

Developmental Research and Programs, Inc. (2000). *Communities That Care prevention strategies: A research guide to what works.* Seattle, WA.

Dishion, T. J., Andrews, D. W., & Crosby, L. (1995). Adolescent boys and their friends in adolescence: Relationship characteristics, quality and interactional process. *Child Development*, 66, 139–151.

_____, Patterson, G. R., & Griesler, P. C. (1994). Peer adaptation in the development of antisocial behavior: A confluence model. In L. R. Huesmann (Ed.), *Aggressive behavior: Current perspectives* (pp. 61–95). New York: Plenum.

Drug Strategies Research Institute. (1998). *Safe schools, safe students: A guide to violence prevention strategies.* Washington, DC.

Dukes, R. L., Ullman, J. B., & Stein, J. A. (1996). Three-year follow-up of Drug Abuse Resistance Education (D.A.R.E.). *Evaluation Review*, 20, 49–66.

Dumas, J. E. (1989). Treating antisocial behavior in children: Child and family approaches. *Clinical Psychology Review*, 9, 197–222.

Elliott, D. S. (1998). Editor's introduction. In D. S. Elliott (Ed.), *Blueprints for violence prevention. Book eight: Multidimensional treatment foster care.* Boulder, CO: Center for the Study and Prevention of Violence.

_____, & Menard, S. (1996). Delinquent friends and delinquent behavior: Temporal and developmental patterns. In J. D. Hawkins (Ed.), *Current theories of crime and deviance* (pp. 28–67). Newbury, CA: Sage Publications.

_____, & Tolan, P. H. (1999). Youth violence, prevention, intervention, and social policy. In D. J. Flannery & C. R. Huff (Eds.), *Youth violence: Prevention, intervention, and social policy* (pp. 3–46). Washington, DC: American Psychiatric Press.

Ennett, S. T., Tobler, N. S., Ringwalt, C. L., & Flewelling, R. L. (1994). How effective is Drug Abuse Resistance Education? A meta-analysis of Project DARE outcome evaluations. *American Journal of Public Health*, 84, 1394–1401.

Fagan, J., Forst, M., & Vivona, T. S. (1989). Youth in prisons and training schools: Perceptions and consequences of the treatment-custody dichotomy. *Juvenile and Family Court*, 40, 1–14.

Falco, M. (1994). *The making of a drug-free America: Programs that work* (rev. ed.). New York: Times Books.

Finckenauer, J. O. (1982). *Scared straight! and the panacea phenomenon.* Englewood Cliffs, NJ: Prentice-Hall.

Flaherty, M. G. (1980). *An assessment of the national incidence of juvenile suicide in adult jails, lockups, and juvenile detention centers.* (Prepared for the U.S. Department of Justice, Office of Justice Programs, Office of Juvenile Justice and Delinquency Prevention). Urbana-Champaign, IL: University of Illinois (Also available: Washington, DC: U.S. Government Printing Office).

Gallup Organization. (1999). *Public opinion poll: Children and violence,* August 24–26, 1999. Available on the World Wide Web: http://www.gallup.com/poll/indicators/indchild_violence.asp

Gendreau, P., Goggin, C., & Smith, P. (1999). The forgotten issue in effective correctional treatment: Program implementation. *International Journal of Offender Therapy and Comparative Criminology,* 43, 180–187.

_____, & Ross, R. R. (1987). Revivification of rehabilitation: Evidence from the 1980s. *Justice Quarterly,* 4, 349–407.

Gottfredson, D. C., Wilson, D. B., & Najaka, S. S. (In press). School-based crime prevention. In D. P. Farrington, L. W. Sherman, & B. Welsh (Eds.), *Evidence-based crime prevention.* London, United Kingdom: Harwood Academic Publishers.

_____. (1997). School-based crime prevention. In L. W. Sherman, D. C. Gottfredson, D. Mackenzie, J. Eck, P. Reuter, & S. Bushway, *Preventing crime: What works, what doesn't, what's promising: A report to the United States Congress* (NCJ 171676, pp. 125–182). Washington, DC: U.S. Department of Justice, Office of Justice Programs.

_____, Gottfredson, D. C., Czeh, E. R., Cantor, D., Crosse, S. B., & Hantman, I. (2000). *National study of delinquency prevention in schools: Summary.* Ellicott City, MD: Gottfredson Associates. [Also available on the World Wide Web: http://www.gottfredson.com/national.htm]

Greenwood, P. W. (1995, unpublished manuscript). The cost-effectiveness of early intervention as a strategy for reducing violent crime. Prepared for the University of California Policy Seminar on Crime Project.

_____, Rydell, C. P., & Model, K. E. (1998). *Diverting children from a life of crime: Measuring costs and benefits* (rev. ed.). Santa Monica, CA: RAND.

Hamilton Fish Institute. (2000). *Effective violence prevention programs.* Available on the World Wide Web: www.hamfish.org/pub/evpp.php3

Hansen, W. B., & McNeal, R. B. (1997). How D.A.R.E. works: An examination of program effects on mediating variables. *Health Education and Behavior,* 24, 165–176.

Howell, J. C. (Ed.). (1995). *Guide for implementing the comprehensive strategy for serious, violent, and chronic juvenile offenders* (NCJ 153681). Washington, DC: U.S. Department of Justice, Office of Justice Programs, Office of Juvenile Justice and Delinquency Prevention. [Also available on the World Wide Web: http://www.ncjrs.org/pdffiles/ guide.pdf]

_____, Krisberg, B., Hawkins, J. D., & Wilson, J. J. (1995). *A sourcebook: Serious, violent, and chronic juvenile offenders.* Thousand Oaks, CA: Sage Publications.

Illinois Center for Violence Prevention. (1998). *Fact Sheets: Cost of violence.* Available on the World Wide Web: http://www.violence-prevention.com/costofviolence.asp

Karoly, L. A., Greenwood, P. W., Rydell, C. P., Chiesa, J., Everingham, S. S., Kilburn, M. R., Hoube, J., & Sander, M. (1998). *Investing in our children: What we know and don't know about the costs and benefits of early childhood interventions.* Santa Monica, CA: RAND.

Kazdin, A. E., Bass, D., Siegel, T., & Thomas, C. (1989). Cognitive-behavioral therapy and relationship therapy in the treatment of children referred for antisocial
behavior. *Journal of Consulting and Clinical Psychology, 57,* 522–535.

Kochis, D. S. (1993). *The effectiveness of DARE: Does it work?* Glassboro, NJ: Rowan
University.

Lewis, R. V. (1983). Scared straight—California style: Evaluation of the San Quentin
squire program. *Criminal Justice and Behavior,* 10, 209–226.

Lipsey, M. W. (1992a). Juvenile delinquency treatment: A meta-analytic inquiry into
the variability of effects. In T. D. Cook, H. Cooper, D. S. Cordray, H. Hartmann,
L. V. Hedges, R. J. Light, T. A. Louis, & F. Mosteller (Eds.), *Meta-analysis for explanation: A casebook* (pp. 83–127). New York: Russell Sage.

_____. (1992b). The effect of treatment of juvenile delinquents: Results from meta-
analysis. In F. Losel, D. Bender, & T. Bliesener (Eds.), *Psychology and law: International perspectives* (pp. 131–143). New York: Walter de Gruyter.

_____, & Wilson, D. B. (1998). Effective intervention for serious juvenile offenders:
A synthesis of research. In R. Loeber & D. P. Farrington (Eds.), *Serious and violent juvenile offenders: Risk factors and successful interventions* (pp. 313–345). Thousand Oaks, CA: Sage Publications.

Lipton, D., Martinson, R., & Wilks, J. (1975). *The effectiveness of correctional treatment: A survey of treatment evaluation studies.* New York: Praeger.

Lochman, J. E. (1992). Cognitive-behavioral intervention with aggressive boys: Three-
year follow-up and preventive effects. *Journal of Consulting and Clinical Psychology,*
60, 426–432.

_____, Burch, P. R., Curry, J. F., & Lampron, L. B. (1984). Treatment and general-
ization effects of cognitive-behavioral and goal-setting interventions with aggressive boys. *Journal of Consulting and Clinical Psychology,* 52, 915–916.

Lonigan, C. J., Elbert, J. C., & Johnson, S. B. (1998). Empirically supported psychosocial interventions for children: An overview. *Journal of Clinical Child Psychology,* 27, 138–145.

McCord, J. (1978). A thirty-year follow-up of treatment effects. *American Psychologist,* 33, 284–289.

Mendel, R. A. (2000). *Less hype, more help: Reducing juvenile crime, what works—and
what doesn't.* Washington, DC: American Youth Policy Forum. [Also available on
the World Wide Web: http://www.aypf.org/mendel/index.html]

Nyre, G. F. (1985). *Final evaluation report, 1984–1985: Project DARE.* Los Angeles:
Evaluation and Training Institute.

_____. (1984). *Evaluation of Project DARE.* Los Angeles: Evaluation and Training
Institute.

O'Leary, K. D., & O'Leary, S. G. (1977). *Classroom management: The successful use of
behavior modification* (2nd ed.). New York: Pergamon Press.

Palumbo, D. J., & Ferguson, J. L. (1995). Evaluating Gang Resistance Education and
Training (G.R.E.A.T.): Is the impact the same as that of Drug Abuse Resistance
Education (D.A.R.E.)? *Evaluation Review,* 19, 597–619.

Patterson, G. R., & Yoerger, K. (1997). A developmental model for late-onset delinquency. In D. W. Osgood (Ed.), *Motivation and delinquency* (Vol. 44, pp. 119–177).
Lincoln, NE: University of Nebraska Press.

Petersilia, J. (1990). Conditions that permit intensive supervision programs to survive. *Crime and Delinquency,* 36, 126–145.

Ringwalt, C. L., Greene, J. M., Ennett, S. T., Iachan, R., Clayton, R. R., & Leukefeld, C. G. (1994). *Past and future direction of the D.A.R.E. program: An evaluation
review.* Research Triangle Park, NC: Research Triangle Institute.

Rocky Mountain Behavioral Science Institute. (1995, Fall). A model for evaluating D.A.R.E. and other prevention programs. *News and Views Newsletter.*

Rosenbaum D. P., Flewelling, R. L., Bailey, S. L., Ringwalt, C. L., & Wilkinson, D. L. (1994). Cops in the classroom: A longitudinal evaluation of Drug Abuse Resistance Education (D.A.R.E.). *Journal of Research in Crime and Delinquency*, 31, 3–31.

_____, & Hanson, G. S. (1998). *Assessing the effects of school-based drug education: A six year multi-level analysis of project D.A.R.E.* Chicago: University of Illinois.

Rotheram, M. J. (1982). Social skills training with underachievers, disruptive, and exceptional children. *Psychology in the Schools*, 19, 532–539.

Sechrest, L. B., White, S. O., & Brown, E. D. (1979). *The rehabilitation of criminal offenders: Problems and prospects.* Washington, DC: National Academy Press.

Sherman, L. W., Gottfredson, D. C., MacKenzie, D. L., Eck, J., Reuter, P., & Bushway, S. D. (1997). *Preventing crime: What works, what doesn't, what's promising. A report to the United States Congress* (NCJ 171676). Washington, DC: U.S. Department of Justice, Office of Justice Programs.

Slavin, R. E. (1990). Achievement effects of ability grouping in secondary schools: A best-evidence synthesis. *Review of Educational Research*, 60, 471–499.

_____. (1989). When does cooperative learning increase student achievement? *Psychological Bulletin*, 94, 429–445.

Thornton, T. N., Craft, C. A., Dahlberg, L. L., Lynch, B. S., & Baer, K. (2000). *Best practices of youth violence prevention: A sourcebook for community action.* Atlanta, GA: Centers for Disease Control and Prevention, National Center for Injury Prevention and Control.

Tolan, P., & Guerra, N. (1994). *What works in reducing adolescent violence: An empirical review of the field.* Boulder, CO: Center for the Study and Prevention of Violence.

Tremblay, R., & Craig, W. (1995). Developmental crime prevention. In M. Tonry & D. P. Farrington (Eds.), *Crime and justice. Vol. 19, Building a safer society: Strategic approaches to crime prevention* (Vol. 19, pp. 151–236). Chicago: University of Chicago Press.

U.S. Department of Health and Human Services. (1999). *Mental health: A report of the Surgeon General.* Rockville, MD: U.S. Department of Health and Human Services, Substance Abuse and Mental Health Services Administration, Center for Mental Health Services, National Institutes of Health, National Institute of Mental Health. [Also available on the World Wide Web: http://www.surgeon-general.gov/library/mentalhealth]

Vito, G. (1984). Developments in shock probation: A review of research findings and policy implications. *Federal Probation*, 48, 22–27.

_____, & Allen, H. E. (1981). Shock probation in Ohio: A comparison of outcomes. *International Journal of Offender Therapy and Comparative Criminology*, 25, 70–75.

Washington State Institute for Public Policy. (1999). *The comparative costs and benefits of programs to reduce crime.* Olympia, WA.

Zagumny, M.J., & Thompson, M.K. (1997). Does D.A.R.E. work? An evaluation in rural Tennessee. *Journal of Alcohol and Drug Education*, 42, 32–41.

Notes

Introduction

1. Schwartz, Wendy. "An Overview of Strategies to Reduce School Violence." Eric Clearinghouse on Urban Education. http://eric-web.tc.columbia.edu/digest/dig115.html .
2. *Ibid.*
3. *Ibid.*
4. Kilpatrick, William. "Why Johnny Can't Tell Right from Wrong." Quoted in Philip F. Vincent, *Rules and Procedures for Character Education* (Chapel Hill, NC: Character Development Group, 1998), vii.
5. *Ibid.*
6. Bennett, William. *The Index of Leading Cultural Indicators: Facts and Figures on the State of American Society* (New York: Simon and Schuster, 1994).
7. Vincent, Philip F. *Rules and Procedures for Character Education* (Chapel Hill, NC: Character Development Group, 1998), 2.
8. McClellan, B. Edward. *Moral Education in America* (New York: Teacher's College Press, 1999), 90.
9. *Ibid.*
10. Vincent, Philip F., editor. *A Gift of Character: The Chattanooga Story.* Also, *Operating Manual for Character Education Programs* (Chapel Hill, NC: Character Development Group, 1998).
11. McClellan, B. Edward, *op. cit.*, 91.

Chapter 1

1. Sears, David O., et al. *Social Psychology*, 10th edition (Englewood Cliffs, N.J.: Prentice-Hall, 2000), 287.
2. Straus, Murray A., et al. *Behind Closed Doors: Violence in the American Family* (Garden City, N.Y.: Doubleday Anchor Books, 1981).
3. "Facts About Violence Among Youth and Violence in Schools." CDC Media Relations, April 21, 1999. http://www.cdc.gov/od/oc/media/fact/violence.htm.
4. "Youth Violence: A Report of the Surgeon General." U.S. Department of Health and Human Services, Office of the Surgeon General, 1999. http://www.mentalhealth.org/youthviolence/. Also see: http://www.cdc.gov/od/oc/media/fact/violence.htm and http://www.cdc.gov/od/oc/media/pressrel/r990421.htm.

5. Butts, Jeffrey. "Youth Violence: Perception Versus Reality." The Urban Institute, a nonpartisan economic and social policy research organization. http://www.urban.org/crime/module/butts/youth_violence.html.

6. "Youth Violence Declines." ABCNews.com., 1999. http://abcnews.go.com/sections/us/DailyNews/youthviolence990804.html.

7. Sears, David O. et al., *op. cit.*, 287–327.

8. Margalit, Avishai. *The Decent Society* (Cambridge, Mass.: Harvard University Press, 1996), 1-6.

9. Selznick, Philip. *The Moral Commonwealth* (Berkeley, Calif.: University of California Press, 1992), 4-14.

10. Dewey, John. *The Quest for Certainty* (1929; reprint, New York: G. P. Putnam's Sons, 1960), 24f.

11. Selznick, Philip, *op. cit.*

12. Barker, R. G. et al. "Frustration and Regression: An Experiment with Young Children." University of Iowa Studies in Child Welfare, 18 (1), 1941.

13. Howland, C. I. and R. R. Sears. "Minor Studies of Aggression: Correlation of Lynchings With Economic Indices." *Journal of Psychology*, 9, 301–310, 1940.

14. Mintz, A. "A Reexamination of Correlations Between Lynchings and Economic Indices." *Journal of Abnormal and Social Psychology*, 41, 154–160, 1946.

15. Shepard, Jon M. *Sociology*, 5th edition (New York: West Publishing Company, 1993), 344.

16. Dollard, J. et al. *Frustration and Aggression* (New Haven, Conn.: Yale University Press, 1939).

17. *Ibid.*

18. Sears, David O. et al. *op. cit.*, 293.

19. *Ibid.*

20. Averill, J. R. "Personal Control Over Aversive Stimuli and Its Relationship to Stress." *Psychological Bulletin*, 80, 286–303, 1973.

21. Sears, David O. et al. *op. cit.*, 287–327.

22. *Ibid.*

23. *Ibid.*

24. Straus, Murray A. "Physical Violence in American Families." In *Sociological Footprints*, 6th edition, Leonard Cargan and Jeanne H. Ballantine, editors (Belmont, Calif.: Wadsworth Publishing Company, 1994), 225–234.

25. Sears, David O. et al. *op. cit.*, 301–303.

26. *Ibid.*

27. Straus, Murray A. "Discipline and Deviance: Physical Punishment of Children and Violence and Other Crimes in Adulthood." In *Sociological Footprints*, 6th edition, Leonard Cargan and Jeanne H. Ballantine, editors (Belmont, Calif.: Wadsworth Publishing Company, 1994), 75–91.

28. *Ibid.*

29. Hester, Joseph P. Bridges: *Building Relationships and Resolving Conflicts* (Chapel Hill, N.C.: New View Publishers, 1995), xii.

Chapter 2

1. Hester, Joseph P. "The Teacher As Leader in the Middle." *The North Carolina League of Middle Schools Journal*, spring 1981.

2. Drucker, Peter. *On the Profession of Management* (Boston: Harvard Business Review Publishing, 1998), 153–154.

3. Selechty, Phillip C. *Schools for the 21st Century, Leadership Imperatives for Educational Reform* (San Francisco: Jossey-Bass Publishers, 1990), see chapter one, 3-17 and chapter four, 49-63.

4. Cashman, Kevin. *Leadership From the Inside Out* (Provo, Utah: Executive Excellence Publishing, 1998).

5. http://www.ed.gov/offices/OESE/SDFS/actguid/intro.html

6. http://www.ed.gov/updates/7priorities/index.html

7. http://www.psea.org/pseafrontpage/news/greenleaf.htm

8. http://www.surgeongeneral.gov/library/youthviolence/report.html

9. http://www.ed.gov/PressReleases/10-1999/wh-1019a.html

10. http://www.ed.gov/offices/OSERS/OSEP/Products/ActionGuide/Action_Guide.pdf

11. http://www.ed.gov/PressReleases/10-1999/wh-1019a.html

12. http://www.house.gov/moore/issue-publicsafety.htm

13. http://www.ed.gov/News/Letters/020211.html

14. http://www.ed.gov/PressReleases/02-2002/02142002.html

15. http://www.michigansafeschools.org/model-conduct-final.htm

16. http://www.state.ny.us/governor/press/aug18_3_98.htm and http://www.senate.state.ny.us/sofl092.html

17. http://www.mhrcc.org/scss/save.html

18. http://www.state.oh.us/CDR/legislation/kentucky.htm

19. http://www.state.in.us/legislative/hdpr/R37_03031999.html

20. http://www.state.ma.us/EOPS/releases/swift_bully.htm

21. http://www.oregonlive.com/news/99/09/st092610.html

22. http://ncinfo.iog.unc.edu/pubs/nclegis/nclegis98/chapternine.html

23. http://www.sen.ca.gov/ftp/sen/sfa/_7sfa06.htm#H3_6_9

24. http://www.tea.state.tx.us/brief/doc4.html#scr79

25. http://www.state.in.us/legislative/hdpr/R25_01192000.html

26. http://eric-web.tc.columbia.edu/digests/dig121.html

27. http://www.accesseric.org/resources/ericreview/vol7no1/federal.html

Chapter 3

1. http://www.surgeongeneral.gov/library/youthviolence/report.html, see: Chapter Five.

2. See the following:

Andrews, D. A. (1994, unpublished manuscript). "An Overview of Treatment Effectiveness: Research and Clinical Principles."

Tolan, P., & Guerra, N. (1994). "What Works in Reducing Adolescent Violence: An Empirical Review of the Field." Boulder, CO: Center for the Study and Prevention of Violence.

3. http://www.surgeongeneral.gov/library/youthviolence/report.html, see: Chapter Five, Part Three: "Scientific Standards for Determining Program Effectiveness."

4. Bry, B. H. (1982). "Reducing the Incidence of Adolescent Problems Through Preventive Intervention: One- and Five-Year Follow-up. *American Journal of Community Psychology*, 10, 265-276.

Bry, B. H., & George, F. E. (1980). "The Preventive Effects of Early Intervention on the Attendance and Grades of Urban Adolescents." Professional Psychology, 2, 252-260.

5. O'Leary, K. D., & O'Leary, S. G. (1977). *Classroom Management: The Successful Use of Behavior Modification* (2nd ed.). New York: Pergamon Press.

6. Slavin, R. E. (1990). "Achievement Effects of Ability Grouping in Secondary Schools: A Best-Evidence Synthesis." *Review of Educational Research*, 60, 471-499.

Slavin, R. E. (1989). When does cooperative learning increase student achievement? Psychological Bulletin, 94, 429-445.

7. http://www.surgeongeneral.gov/library/youthviolence/report.html, see: Chapter Five, Part Four: "Strategies and Programs: Model, Promising, and Does Not Work."

8. http://www.surgeongeneral.gov/library/youthviolence/report.html, see: Chapter Five, Part Four: "Strategies and Programs: Model, Promising, and Does Not Work – Tertiary Prevention: Violent or Seriously Delinquent Youths."

9. Lipsey, M. W. (1992b). "The Effect of Treatment of Juvenile Delinquents: Results from Meta-Analysis." In F. Losel, D. Bender, & T. Bliesener (Eds.), *Psychology and Law: International Perspectives* (pp. 131-143). New York: Walter de Gruyter.

10. Gendreau, P., & Ross, R. R. (1987). "Revivification of Rehabilitation: Evidence from the 1980s." *Justice Quarterly*, 4, 349-407.

11. Tremblay, R., & Craig, W. (1995). "Developmental Crime Prevention." In M. Tonry & D. P. Farrington (Eds.), *Crime and Justice*. Vol. 19, "Building a Safer Society: Strategic Approaches to Crime Prevention" (Vol. 19, pp. 151-236). Chicago: University of Chicago Press.

12. McCord, J. (1978). "A Thirty-Year Follow-up of Treatment Effects." *American Psychologist*, 33, 284-289.

13. Lipsey, M. W. (1992b). "The Effect of Treatment of Juvenile Delinquents: Results from Meta-Analysis." In F. Losel, D. Bender, & T. Bliesener (Eds.), *Psychology and Law: International Perspectives* (pp. 131-143). New York: Walter de Gruyter.

14. Andrews, D. A., Zinger, I., Hoge, R. D., Bonta, J., Gendreau, P., & Cullen, F. T. (1990). "A Clinically Relevant and Psychologically Informed Meta-Analysis." *Criminology*, 28, 369-387.

15. http://www.surgeongeneral.gov/library/youthviolence/report.html, see: Chapter Five, Conclusions.

16. Petersilia, J. (1990). "Conditions That Permit Intensive Supervision Programs to Survive." *Crime and Delinquency*, 36, 126-145.

17. Thornton, T. N., Craft, C. A., Dahlberg, L. L., Lynch, B. S., & Baer, K. (2000). "Best Practices of Youth Violence Prevention: A Sourcebook for Community Action." Atlanta, GA: Centers for Disease Control and Prevention, National Center for Injury Prevention and Control.

18. *Ibid.*

19. Gottfredson, D. C., Wilson, D. B., & Najaka, S. S. (In press). "School-Based Crime Prevention." In D. P. Farrington, L. W. Sherman, & B. Welsh (Eds.), Evidence-based crime prevention. London, United Kingdom: Harwood Academic Publishers.

20. http://www.eric.ed.gov/resources/ericreview/vol7no1/contents.html. Also see Urban Education Web (UEweb): School Safety at http://eric-web.tc.columbia.edu/administration/safety/. This is an excellent resource on school safety issues with three pages of specific topics connected to their designated websites.

21. http://www.eric.ed.gov/resources/ericreview/vol7no1/commctr.html.

22. http://www.eric.ed.gov/resources/ericreview/vol7no1/evaluate.html.

23. http://www.eric.ed.gov/resources/ericreview/vol7no1/design.html.

24. http://www.eric.ed.gov/resources/ericreview/vol7no1/behavior.html.

25. http://www.eric.ed.gov/resources/ericreview/vol7no1/ethnic.html.

26. http://www.eric.ed.gov/resources/ericreview/vol7no1/conflict.html.
27. http://www.mentalhealth.org/schoolviolence/about.asp.
28. http://eric-web.tc.columbia.edu/digests/dig115.html.
29. http://nces.ed.gov/pubs98/violence/index.html.

Chapter 4

1. "Creating Safe and Drug-Free Schools, An Action Guide, April 1997" http://www.ed.gov/offices/OESE/SDFS/actguid/index.html
2. "Preventing Violence in Schools" http://eric-web.tc.columbia.edu/monographs/uds107/preventing_contents.html.
3. ERIC Review: "School Safety: A Collaborative Effort" http://www.eric.ed.gov/resources/ericreview/vol7no1/contents.html.
4. http://www.eric.ed.gov/resources/ericreview/vol7no1/contents.html.
5. "School Violence, Risk, Preventive Intervention and Policy" http://eric-web.tc.columbia.edu/monographs/uds109/illustration.html
6. Safe Schools Model Homepage http://www.safeschoolmodel.org/Our_Model/our_model.html

Chapter 5

1. Hester, Joseph P. "The Teacher As Leader." *The North Carolina Middle School Association Journal*, Volume 21, Spring 2001, pp. 38-43. See also, Joseph P. Hester, *Talking It Over: A Workbook for Character Education* (Lanham, Maryland: A ScarecrowEducation Book, 2002).
2. Schlechty, Phillip C. *Schools for the 21st Century: Leadership Imperatives for Educational Reform* (San Francisco: Jossey-Bass Publishers, 1990).
3. Drucker, Peter. *On the Profession of Management* (Boston: Harvard Business Review Publishing, 1998).
4. Bennis, Warren. *On Becoming a Leader* (Reading, Massachusetts: Perseus Books, 1994). See also: Peter M. Senge. *The Fifth Discipline: The Art and Practice of the Learning Organization* (New York: Doubleday Currency, 1990), and Ken Blanchard and Michael O'Connor, *Managing by Values* (San Francisco: Berrett-Koehler Publishers, 1997).
5. Young, H. Darrell and Joseph P. Hester. *Building a Leadership Culture: A Training Guide* (Chapel Hill: Character Development Publishing, 2000).
6. Cashman, Kevin. *Leadership From the Inside Out* (Provo, Utah: Executive Excellence Publishing, 1998).
7. Drucker, Peter. *op. cit.*
8. Cargan, Leonard and Jeanne H. Ballantine. *Sociological Footprints*, 6th edition (Belmont, California: Wadsworth Publishing Company, 1994).
9. Havener, Cliff. *Meaning* (Edina, Minnesota: Beaver's Pond Press, Inc., 1999). See chapter 5, 71-88.
10. Report of the Carnegie Council on Adolescent Development, "Turning Points" (Menlo Park, California: Carnegie Foundation for the Advancement of Teaching, 1989).
11. Hester, Joseph P. and Philip F. Vincent. *Philosophy For Young Thinkers* (Monroe, New York: Trillium Press, 1983-1989).

12. Botstein, Leon. *Jefferson's Children* (New York: Doubleday, 1997).

13. Lynch, Aaron. *Thought Contagion* (New York: Basic Books, 1996).

14. Wilson, James Q. *The Moral Sense* (New York: The Free Press, 1993).

15. Hester, Joseph P. *Teaching for Thinking* (Durham, North Carolina: Carolina Academic Press, 1994).

16. Hester, Joseph P. *Bridges: Building Relationships and Resolving Conflicts* (Chapel Hill, North Carolina: New View Publishers, 1995).

17. Hyerle, David. *Thinking Maps Training Manual* (Cary, North Carolina: Innovative Sciences, Inc., 1993).

18. Gouinlock, James. *The Moral Writings of John Dewey* (Amherst, New York: Prometheus Books, 1994).

19. Vincent, Philip F. *Developing Character in Students*, 2nd edition (Chapel Hill, North Carolina: Character Development Publishing, 1999).

20. Conrad, D. and D. Hedin. "High School Community Service: A Review of Research and Programs" (Washington, D.C.: National Center on Effective Secondary Schools, U.S. Department of Education, Office of Educational Research and Improvement; and Madison, Wisconsin: Wisconsin Center for Educational Research, School of Education, University of Wisconsin, 1989).

21. Vincent, Philip F. *op. cit.*

22. Hester, Joseph P. *Talking It Over: A Workbook for Character Education* (Lanham, Maryland: A ScarecrowEducation Book, 2002).

Chapter 6

The Website references for chapter six are contained in the alphabetical listing of school safety resources, organizations, and publications.

Bibliography

Andrews, D. A. (1994, unpublished manuscript). "An Overview of Treatment Effectiveness: Research and Clinical Principles."

_____, Zinger, I., Hoge, R. D., Bonta, J., Gendreau, P., & Cullen, F. T. (1990). "A Clinically Relevant and Psychologically Informed Meta-Analysis." *Criminology, 28,* 369–387.

Aniskiewicz, R. E., & Wysong, E. E. (1990). "Evaluating DARE: Drug Education and the Multiple Meanings of Success." *Policy Studies Review, 9,* 727–747.

Aos, S., Phipps, P. V., Barnoski, R., & Leib, R. (1999). "The Comparative Costs and Benefits of Programs to Reduce Crime: A Review of National Research Findings with Implications for Washington State" (Report No. 99–05–1202). Olympia, WA: Washington State Institute for Public Policy. [Also available on the World Wide Web: http://www.wsipp.wa.gov/crime/costben.html].

Arbuthnot, J., & Gordon, D. A. (1986). "Behavioral and Cognitive Effects of a Moral Reasoning Development Intervention for High-Risk Behavior-Disordered Adolescents." *Journal of Consulting and Clinical Psychology, 54,* 208–216.

Averill, J. R. "Personal Control Over Aversive Stimuli and Its Relationship to Stress." *Psychological Bulletin, 80,* 286–303, 1973.

Barker, R. G. et al. "Frustration and Regression: An Experiment with Young Children." *University of Iowa Studies in Child Welfare, 18* (1), 1941.

Bennett, William. *The Index of Leading Cultural Indicators: Facts and Figures on the State of American Society* (New York: Simon and Schuster, 1994).

Bennis, Warren. *On Becoming a Leader* (Reading, Massachusetts: Perseus Books, 1994). See also: Peter M. Senge, *The Fifth Discipline: The Art and Practice of the Learning Organization* (New York: Doubleday Currency, 1990) and Ken Blanchard and Michael O'Connor, *Managing by Values* (San Francisco: Berrett-Koehler Publishers, 1997).

Bishop, D. (2000). "Juvenile Offenders in the Adult Criminal Justice System." In M. Tonry (Ed.), *Youth Violence. Crime and Justice: A Review of Research* (Vol. 27, pp. 81–168). Chicago: University of Chicago Press.

_____, & Frazier, C. (2000). "The Consequences of Waiver." In J. Fagan & F. E. Zimring (Eds.), *The Changing Borders of Juvenile Justice: Transfer of Adolescents to the Criminal Court* (pp. 227–276). Chicago: University of Chicago Press.

Botstein, Leon. *Jefferson's Children* (New York: Doubleday, 1997).

Boudouris, J., & Turnbull, B. W. (1985). "Shock Probation in Iowa." *Journal of Offender Counseling, Services and Rehabilitation, 9,* 53–67.

Bry, B. H. (1982). "Reducing the Incidence of Adolescent Problems Through Preventive Intervention: One- and Five-Year Follow-Up." *American Journal of Community Psychology*, 10, 265–276.

____, & George, F. E. (1980). "The Preventive Effects of Early Intervention on the Attendance and Grades of Urban Adolescents." *Professional Psychology*, 2, 252–260.

____, & ____. (1979). "Evaluating and Improving Prevention Programs: A Strategy From Drug Abuse." *Evaluation and Program Planning*, 2, 127–136.

Buckner, J. C., & Chesney-Lind, M. (1983). "Dramatic Cures for Juvenile Crime: An Evaluation of a Prison-run Delinquency Prevention Program." *Criminal Justice and Behavior*, 10, 227–247.

Butts, Jeffrey. "Youth Violence: Perception Versus Reality." The Urban Institute, a nonpartisan economic and social policy research organization. See: http://www.urban.org/crime/module/butts/youth_violence.html.

Cargan, Leonard and Jeanne H. Ballantine. *Sociological Footprints*, 6th edition (Belmont, California: Wadsworth Publishing Company, 1994).

Cashman, Kevin. *Leadership from the Inside Out* (Provo, Utah: Executive Excellence Publishing, 1998).

Center for Substance Abuse Prevention. (2000). CSAP's model programs. Available on the World Wide Web: http://www.samhsa.gov/csap/modelprograms/default.htm.

Center for the Study and Prevention of Violence. (1998). *CSPV Position Summary: D.A.R.E. Program.* Available on the World Wide Web: http://www.colorado.edu/cspv/positions/position3.html.

Chamberlain, P., & Mihalic, S. F. (1998). "Multi-Dimensional Treatment Foster Care." In D. S. Elliott (Series Ed.), *Blueprints for Violence Prevention. Multi-Dimensional Treatment Foster Care*. Boulder, CO: Center for the Study and Prevention of Violence, Institute of Behavioral Sciences, University of Colorado at Boulder.

Chandler, M. J. (1993). "Egocentrism and Antisocial Behavior: The Assessment and Training of Social Perspective-Taking Skills." *Developmental Psychology*, 9, 326–332.

Cohen, P. A., Kulik, J. A., & Kulik, C. L. (1982). "Educational Outcomes of Tutoring: A Meta-Analysis of Findings." *American Educational Research Journal*, 19, 237–248.

Conrad, D. and D. Hedin. "High School Community Service: A Review of Research and Programs" (Washington, D.C.: National Center on Effective Secondary Schools, U.S. Department of Education, Office of Educational Research and Improvement; and Madison, Wisconsin: Wisconsin Center for Educational Research, School of Education, University of Wisconsin, 1989).

"Creating Safe and Drug-Free Schools: An Action Guide, April 1997." http://www.ed.gov/offices/OESE/SDFS/actguid/index.html.

Dejong, W. (1987). "A Short-Term Evaluation of Project DARE (Drug Abuse Resistance Education): Preliminary Indicators of Effectiveness." *Journal of Drug Education*, 17, 279–294.

Developmental Research and Programs, Inc. (2000). *Communities That Care. Prevention Strategies: A Research Guide to What Works*. Seattle, WA.

Dewey, John. *The Quest for Certainty* (1929; reprint, New York: G. P. Putnam's Sons, 1960).

Dishion, T. J., Andrews, D. W., & Crosby, L. (1995). "Adolescent Boys and Their Friends in Adolescence: Relationship Characteristics, Quality and Interactional Process." *Child Development*, 66, 139–151.

____, Patterson, G. R., & Griesler, P. C. (1994). "Peer Adaptation in the Development of Antisocial Behavior: A Confluence Model." In L. R. Huesmann (Ed.), *Aggressive Behavior: Current Perspectives* (pp. 61–95). New York: Plenum.

Dollard, J. et al. *Frustration and Aggression* (New Haven, Conn.: Yale University Press, 1939).

Drucker, Peter. *On the Profession of Management* (Boston: Harvard Business Review Publishing, 1998).

Drug Strategies Research Institute. (1998). *Safe Schools, Safe Students: A Guide to Violence Prevention Strategies.* Washington, DC.

Dukes, R. L., Ullman, J. B., & Stein, J. A. (1996). "Three-Year Follow-Up of Drug Abuse Resistance Education (D.A.R.E.)." *Evaluation Review,* 20, 49–66.

Dumas, J. E. (1989). "Treating Antisocial Behavior in Children: Child and Family Approaches." *Clinical Psychology Review,* 9, 197–222.

Elliott, D. S. (1998). Editor's introduction. In D. S. Elliott (Ed.), *Blueprints for Violence Prevention. Book Eight: Multidimensional Treatment Foster Care.* Boulder, CO: Center for the Study and Prevention of Violence.

_____, & Menard, S. (1996). "Delinquent Friends and Delinquent Behavior: Temporal and Developmental Patterns." In J. D. Hawkins (Ed.), *Current Theories of Crime and Deviance* (pp. 28–67). Newbury, CA: Sage Publications.

_____, & Tolan, P. H. (1999). "Youth Violence, Prevention, Intervention, and Social Policy." In D. J. Flannery & C. R. Huff (Eds.), *Youth Violence: Prevention, Intervention, and Social Policy* (pp. 3–46). Washington, DC: American Psychiatric Press.

Ennett, S. T., Tobler, N. S., Ringwalt, C. L., & Flewelling, R. L. (1994). "How Effective Is Drug Abuse Resistance Education? A Meta-Analysis of Project DARE Outcome Evaluations." *American Journal of Public Health,* 84, 1394–1401.

ERIC Review: "School Safety: A Collaborative Effort" http://www.eric.ed.gov/resources/ericreview/vol7no1/contents.html.

"Facts About Violence Among Youth and Violence in Schools." CDC Media Relations, April 21, 1999. http://www.cdc.gov/od/oc/media/fact/violence.htm.

Fagan, J., Forst, M., & Vivona, T. S. (1989). "Youth in Prisons and Training Schools: Perceptions and Consequences of the Treatment-Custody Dichotomy." *Juvenile and Family Court,* 40, 1–14.

Falco, M. (1994). *The Making of a Drug-Free America: Programs That Work* (rev. ed.). New York: Times Books.

Finckenauer, J. O. (1982). *Scared Straight! And the Panacea Phenomenon.* Englewood Cliffs, NJ: Prentice-Hall.

Flaherty, M. G. (1980). *An Assessment of the National Incidence of Juvenile Suicide in Adult Jails, Lockups, and Juvenile Detention Centers.* (Prepared for the U.S. Department of Justice, Office of Justice Programs, Office of Juvenile Justice and Delinquency Prevention). Urbana-Champaign, IL: University of Illinois (Also available: Washington, DC: U.S. Government Printing Office).

Gallup Organization. (1999). *Public Opinion Poll: Children and Violence,* August 24–26, 1999. Available on the World Wide Web: http://www.gallup.com/poll/indicators/indchild_violence.asp.

Gendreau, P., & Ross, R. R. (1987). "Revivification of Rehabilitation: Evidence from the 1980s." *Justice Quarterly,* 4, 349–407.

_____, Goggin, C., & Smith, P. (1999). "The Forgotten Issue in Effective Correctional Treatment: Program Implementation." *International Journal of Offender Therapy and Comparative Criminology,* 43, 180–187.

Gottfredson, D. C. (1997). "School-Based Crime Prevention." In L. W. Sherman, D. C. Gottfredson, D. Mackenzie, J. Eck, P. Reuter, & S. Bushway, *Preventing Crime: What Works, What Doesn't, What's Promising: A Report to the United States Congress* (NCJ 171676, pp. 125–182). Washington, DC: U.S. Department of Justice, Office of Justice Programs.

_____, Wilson, D. B., & Najaka, S. S. (In press). "School-Based Crime Prevention." In D. P. Farrington, L. W. Sherman, & B. Welsh (Eds.), *Evidence-Based Crime Prevention.* London, United Kingdom: Harwood Academic Publishers.

_____, Gottfredson, D. C., Czeh, E. R., Cantor, D., Crosse, S. B., & Hantman, I. (2000). *National Study of Delinquency Prevention in Schools: Summary.* Ellicott City, MD: Gottfredson Associates. [Also available on the World Wide Web: http://www. gottfredson.com/national.htm]

Gouinlock, James. *The Moral Writings of John Dewey* (Amherst, New York: Prometheus Books, 1994).

Greenwood, P. W. (1995, unpublished manuscript). "The Cost-Effectiveness of Early Intervention as a Strategy for Reducing Violent Crime." Prepared for the University of California Policy Seminar on Crime Project.

_____, Rydell, C. P., & Model, K. E. (1998). *Diverting Children from a Life of Crime: Measuring Costs and Benefits* (rev. ed.). Santa Monica, CA: RAND.

Hamilton Fish Institute. (2000). *Effective Violence Prevention Programs.* Available on the World Wide Web: www.hamfish.org/pub/evpp.php3.

Hansen, W. B., & McNeal, R. B. (1997). "How D.A.R.E. Works: An Examination of Program Effects on Mediating Variables." *Health Education and Behavior,* 24, 165–176.

Havener, Cliff. *Meaning* (Edina, Minnesota: Beaver's Pond Press, Inc., 1999). See chapter 5, 71–88.

Hester, Joseph P. *Bridges: Building Relationships and Resolving Conflicts* (Chapel Hill, North Carolina: New View Publishers, 1995).

_____. *Talking It Over: A Workbook for Character Education* (Lanham, Maryland: A ScarecrowEducation Book, 2002).

_____. "The Teacher as Leader in the Middle." *The North Carolina League of Middle Schools Journal,* spring 1981.

_____. *Teaching for Thinking* (Durham, North Carolina: Carolina Academic Press, 1994).

_____. and Philip F. Vincent. *Philosophy for Young Thinkers* (Monroe, New York: Trillium Press, 1983–1989).

Howell, J. C. (Ed.). (1995). *Guide for Implementing the Comprehensive Strategy for Serious, Violent, and Chronic Juvenile Offenders* (NCJ 153681). Washington, DC: U.S. Department of Justice, Office of Justice Programs, Office of Juvenile Justice and Delinquency Prevention. [Also available on the World Wide Web: http://www. ncjrs.org/pdffiles/ guide.pdf]

_____, Krisberg, B., Hawkins, J. D., & Wilson, J. J. (1995). *A Sourcebook: Serious, Violent, and Chronic Juvenile Offenders.* Thousand Oaks, CA: Sage Publications.

Howland, C. I. and R. R. Sears. "Minor Studies of Aggression: Correlation of Lynchings With Economic Indices." *Journal of Psychology,* 9, 301–310, 1940.

Hyerle, David. *Thinking Maps Training Manual* (Cary, North Carolina: Innovative Sciences, Inc., 1993).

Illinois Center for Violence Prevention. (1998). *Fact Sheets: Cost of Violence.* Available on the World Wide Web: http://www.violence-prevention.com/costofviolence. asp.

Karoly, L. A., Greenwood, P. W., Rydell, C. P., Chiesa, J., Everingham, S. S., Kilburn, M. R., Hoube, J., & Sander, M. (1998). *Investing in Our Children: What We Know and Don't Know About the Costs and Benefits of Early Childhood Interventions.* Santa Monica, CA: RAND.

Kazdin, A. E., Bass, D., Siegel, T., & Thomas, C. (1989). "Cognitive-Behavioral Therapy and Relationship Therapy in the Treatment of Children Referred for Antisocial Behavior." *Journal of Consulting and Clinical Psychology,* 57, 522–535.

Kilpatrick, William. *Why Johnny Can't Tell Right from Wrong.* Quoted in Philip F. Vincent. *Rules and Procedures for Character Education* (Chapel Hill, NC: Character Development Group, 1998).

Kochis, D. S. (1993). *The Effectiveness of DARE: Does It Work?* Glassboro, NJ: Rowan University.

Lewis, R. V. (1983). "Scared Straight—California Style: Evaluation of the San Quentin Squire Program." *Criminal Justice and Behavior,* 10, 209–226.

Lipsey, M. W. (1992a). "Juvenile Delinquency Treatment: A Meta-Analytic Inquiry Into the Variability of Effects." In T. D. Cook, H. Cooper, D. S. Cordray, H. Hartmann, L. V. Hedges, R. J. Light, T. A. Louis, & F. Mosteller (Eds.), *Meta-Analysis for Explanation: A Casebook* (pp. 83–127). New York: Russell Sage.

_____. (1992b). "The Effect of Treatment of Juvenile Delinquents: Results from Meta-Analysis." In F. Losel, D. Bender, & T. Bliesener (Eds.), *Psychology and Law: International Perspectives* (pp. 131–143). New York: Walter de Gruyter.

_____, & Wilson, D. B. (1998). "Effective Intervention for Serious Juvenile Offenders: A Synthesis of Research." In R. Loeber & D. P. Farrington (Eds.), *Serious and Violent Juvenile Offenders: Risk Factors and Successful Interventions* (pp. 313–345). Thousand Oaks, CA: Sage Publications.

Lipton, D., Martinson, R., & Wilks, J. (1975). *The Effectiveness of Correctional Treatment: A Survey of Treatment Evaluation Studies.* New York: Praeger.

Lochman, J. E. (1992). "Cognitive-Behavioral Intervention with Aggressive Boys: Three-Year Follow-Up and Preventive Effects." *Journal of Consulting and Clinical Psychology,* 60, 426–432.

_____, Burch, P. R., Curry, J. F., & Lampron, L. B. (1984). "Treatment and Generalization Effects of Cognitive-Behavioral and Goal-Setting Interventions with Aggressive Boys." *Journal of Consulting and Clinical Psychology,* 52, 915–916.

Lonigan, C. J., Elbert, J. C., & Johnson, S. B. (1998). "Empirically Supported Psychosocial Interventions for Children: An Overview." *Journal of Clinical Child Psychology,* 27, 138–145.

Lynch, Aaron. *Thought Contagion* (New York: Basic Books, 1996).

McClellan, B. Edward. *Moral Education in America* (New York: Teacher's College Press, 1999), 90.

McCord, J. (1978). "A Thirty-Year Follow-Up of Treatment Effects." *American Psychologist,* 33, 284–289.

Margalit, Avishai. *The Decent Society* (Cambridge, Mass: Harvard University Press, 1996).

Mendel, R. A. (2000). *Less Hype, More Help: Reducing Juvenile Crime, What Works—and What Doesn't.* Washington, DC: American Youth Policy Forum. [Also available on the World Wide Web: http://www.aypf.org/mendel/index.html].

Mintz, A. "A Reexamination of Correlations Between Lynchings and Economic Indices." *Journal of Abnormal and Social Psychology,* 41, 154–160, 1946.

Nyre, G. F. (1984). *Evaluation of Project DARE.* Los Angeles: Evaluation and Training Institute.

_____. (1985). *Final Evaluation Report, 1984–1985: Project DARE.* Los Angeles: Evaluation and Training Institute.

O'Leary, K. D., & O'Leary, S. G. (1977). *Classroom Management: The Successful Use of Behavior Modification* (2nd ed.). New York: Pergamon Press.

Palumbo, D. J., & Ferguson, J. L. (1995). "Evaluating Gang Resistance Education and Training (G.R.E.A.T.): Is the Impact the Same as That of Drug Abuse Resistance Education (D.A.R.E.)?" *Evaluation Review,* 19, 597–619.

Patterson, G. R., & Yoerger, K. (1997). A Developmental Model for Late-Onset Delinquency." In D. W. Osgood (Ed.), *Motivation and Delinquency* (Vol. 44, pp. 119–177). Lincoln, NE: University of Nebraska Press, 1997.

Petersilia, J. (1990). "Conditions That Permit Intensive Supervision Programs to Survive." *Crime and Delinquency,* 36, 126–145.

Report of the Carnegie Council on Adolescent Development, "Turning Points" (Menlo Park, California: Carnegie Foundation for the Advancement of Teaching, 1989).

Ringwalt, C. L., Greene, J. M., Ennett, S. T., Iachan, R., Clayton, R. R., & Leukefeld, C. G. (1994). *Past and Future Direction of the D.A.R.E. Program: An Evaluation Review.* Research Triangle Park, NC: Research Triangle Institute.

Rocky Mountain Behavioral Science Institute. (1995, Fall). "A Model for Evaluating D.A.R.E. and Other Prevention Programs." *News and Views Newsletter.*

Rosenbaum D. P., Flewelling, R. L., Bailey, S. L., Ringwalt, C. L., & Wilkinson, D. L. (1994). "Cops in the Classroom: A Longitudinal Evaluation of Drug Abuse Resistance Education (D.A.R.E.)." *Journal of Research in Crime and Delinquency,* 31, 3–31.

_____, & Hanson, G. S. (1998). *Assessing the Effects of School-Based Drug Education: A Six Year Multi-Level Analysis of Project D.A.R.E.* Chicago: University of Illinois.

Rotheram, M. J. (1982). "Social Skills Training With Underachievers, Disruptive, and Exceptional Children." *Psychology in the Schools,* 19, 532–539.

"School Violence, Risk, Preventive Intervention and Policy." http://eric-web.tc. columbia.edu/monographs/uds109/illustration.html.

Schwartz, Wendy. "An Overview of Strategies to Reduce School Violence." ERIC Clearinghouse on Urban Education. http://eric-web.tc.columbia.edu/digest/dig115 .html.

Sears, David O. et al. *Social Psychology,* 10th edition (Englewood Cliffs, New Jersey: Prentice Hall, Inc., 2000).

Sechrest, L. B., White, S. O., & Brown, E. D. (1979). *The Rehabilitation of Criminal Offenders: Problems and Prospects.* Washington, DC: National Academy Press.

Selechty, Phillip C. *Schools for the 21st Century, Leadership Imperatives for Educational Reform* (San Francisco: Jossey-Bass Publishers, 1990).

Selznick, Philip. *The Moral Commonwealth* (Berkeley, Calif.: University of California Press, 1992).

Shepard, Jon M. *Sociology,* 5th edition (New York: West Publishing Company, 1993), 344.

Sherman, L. W., Gottfredson, D. C., MacKenzie, D. L., Eck, J., Reuter, P., & Bushway, S. D. (1997). *Preventing Crime: What Works, What Doesn't, What's Promising. A Report to the United States Congress* (NCJ 171676). Washington, DC: U.S. Department of Justice, Office of Justice Programs.

Slavin, R. E. (1990). "Achievement Effects of Ability Grouping in Secondary Schools: A Best-Evidence Synthesis." *Review of Educational Research,* 60, 471–499.

_____. (1989). "When Does Cooperative Learning Increase Student Achievement?" *Psychological Bulletin,* 94, 429–445.

Straus, Murray A. "Discipline and Deviance: Physical Punishment of Children and Violence and Other Crimes in Adulthood." In *Sociological Footprints,* 6th edition, Leonard Cargan and Jeanne H. Ballantine, editors (Belmont, Calif.: Wadsworth Publishing Company, 1994).

_____. "Physical Violence in American Families." In *Sociological Footprints,* 6th edition, Leonard Cargan and Jeanne H. Ballantine, editors (Belmont, Calif.: Wadsworth Publishing Company, 1994).

_____. et al. *Behind Closed Doors: Violence in the American Family* (Garden City, New Jersey: Doubleday Anchor Books, 1981).

Thornton, T. N., Craft, C. A., Dahlberg, L. L., Lynch, B. S., & Baer, K. (2000). *Best Practices of Youth Violence Prevention: A Sourcebook for Community Action.* Atlanta, GA: Centers for Disease Control and Prevention, National Center for Injury Prevention and Control.

Tolan, P., & Guerra, N. (1994). *What Works in Reducing Adolescent Violence: An Empirical Review of the Field.* Boulder, CO: Center for the Study and Prevention of Violence.

Tremblay, R., & Craig, W. (1995). "Developmental Crime Prevention." In M. Tonry & D. P. Farrington (Eds.), *Crime and Justice. Vol. 19, Building a Safer Society: Strategic Approaches to Crime Prevention* (Vol. 19, pp. 151–236). Chicago: University of Chicago Press.

U.S. Department of Health and Human Services. (1999). *Mental Health: A Report of the Surgeon General.* Rockville, MD: U.S. Department of Health and Human Services, Substance Abuse and Mental Health Services Administration, Center for Mental Health Services, National Institutes of Health, National Institute of Mental Health. [Also available on the World Wide Web: http://www.surgeon-general.gov/library/mentalhealth].

Vincent, Philip F. *Developing Character in Students,* 2nd edition (Chapel Hill, North Carolina: Character Development Publishing, 1999).

_____. *Rules and Procedures for Character Education* (Chapel Hill, NC: Character Development Group, 1998).

_____, ed. *A Gift of Character: The Chattanooga Story.* Also, *Operating Manual for Character Education Programs* (Chapel Hill, NC: Character Development Group, 1998).

Vito, G. (1984). "Developments in Shock Probation: A Review of Research Findings and Policy Implications." *Federal Probation,* 48, 22–27.

_____, & Allen, H. E. (1981). "Shock Probation in Ohio: A Comparison of Outcomes." *International Journal of Offender Therapy and Comparative Criminology,* 25, 70–75.

Washington State Institute for Public Policy. (1999). *The Comparative Costs and Benefits of Programs to Reduce Crime.* Olympia, WA.

Wilson, James Q. *The Moral Sense* (New York: The Free Press, 1993).

Young, H. Darrell and Joseph P. Hester. *Building a Leadership Culture: A Training Guide* (Chapel Hill: Character Development Publishing, 2000).

"Youth Violence: A Report of the Surgeon General." U. S. Department of Health and Human Services, Office of the Surgeon General, 1999. http://www.mental-health.org/youthviolence/. See also: http://www.cdc.gov/od/oc/media/fact/violence.htm and http://www.cdc.gov/od/oc/media/pressrel/r990421.htm.

Zagumny, M.J., & Thompson, M.K. (1997). "Does D.A.R.E. Work? An Evaluation in Rural Tennessee." *Journal of Alcohol and Drug Education,* 42, 32–41.

Websites

http://eric-web.tc.columbia.edu/digests/dig115.html.
http://eric-web.tc.columbia.edu/digests/dig121.html
http://eric-web.tc.columbia.edu/monographs/uds107/preventing_contents.html.
http://nces.ed.gov/pubs98/violence/index.html.
http://ncinfo.iog.unc.edu/pubs/nclegis/nclegis98/chapternine.html
http://www.accesseric.org/resources/ericreview/vol7no1/federal.html
http://www.ed.gov/News/Letters/020211.html
http://www.ed.gov/offices/OESE/SDFS/actguid/intro.html
http://www.ed.gov/offices/OSERS/OSEP/Products/ActionGuide/Action_Guide.pdf
http://www.ed.gov/PressReleases/02-2002/02142002.html
http://www.ed.gov/PressReleases/10-1999/wh-1019a.html
http://www.ed.gov/PressReleases/10-1999/wh-1019a.html

http://www.ed.gov/updates/7priorities/index.html
http://www.eric.ed.gov/resources/ericreview/vol7no1/behavior.html.
http://www.eric.ed.gov/resources/ericreview/vol7no1/commctr.html.
http://www.eric.ed.gov/resources/ericreview/vol7no1/conflict.html.
http://www.eric.ed.gov/resources/ericreview/vol7no1/contents.html.
http://www.eric.ed.gov/resources/ericreview/vol7no1/design.html.
http://www.eric.ed.gov/resources/ericreview/vol7no1/ethnic.html.
http://www.eric.ed.gov/resources/ericreview/vol7no1/evaluate.html.
http://www.house.gov/moore/issue-publicsafety.htm
http://www.mentalhealth.org/schoolviolence/about.asp.
http://www.mhrcc.org/scss/save.html
http://www.michigansafeschools.org/model-conduct-final.htm
http://www.oregonlive.com/news/99/09/st092610.html
http://www.psea.org/pseafrontpage/news/greenleaf.htm
http://www.safeschoolmodel.org/Our_Model/our_model.html
http://www.sen.ca.gov/ftp/sen/sfa/_7sfa06.htm#H3_6_9
http://www.state.in.us/legislative/hdpr/R25_01192000.html
http://www.state.in.us/legislative/hdpr/R37_03031999.html
http://www.state.ma.us/EOPS/releases/swift_bully.htm
http://www.state.ny.us/governor/press/aug18_3_98.htm and http://www.senate.state.
   ny.us/sofl092.html
http://www.state.oh.us/CDR/legislation/kentucky.htm
http://www.surgeongeneral.gov/library/youthviolence/report.html
http://www.tea.state.tx.us/brief/doc4.html#scr79

Index